W9-ADZ-768

THE MARSHALL CAVENDISH ☆ ☆ ☆ ILLUSTRATED ☆ ☆ ☆ ENCYCLOPEDIA OF WORLD WAR II

VOLUME 17

THE MARSHALL CAVENDISH ☆ ☆ ☆ ILLUSTRATED ☆ ☆ ☆ ENCYCLOPEDIA OF WORLD WAR II

Based on the original text by
Lieutenant Colonel Eddy Bauer

CONSULTANT EDITOR

Brigadier General James L. Collins, Jr., U.S.A.

CHIEF OF MILITARY HISTORY,
DEPARTMENT OF THE ARMY

MARSHALL CAVENDISH CORPORATION/NEW YORK

CONTENTS

Chapter 144 The Allies Confer 2241

THE QUEBEC CONFERENCE
Occupied Germany
The Morgenthau Plan
Churchill's opinion alters
Eisenhower's view: "silly and criminal"
German propaganda benefits

THE MOSCOW CONFERENCE
Churchill's initiative
Spheres of influence
Tito goes it alone
Eden versus Molotov
Poles in exile
Combined Polish government?
Conduct of the war
Violate Swiss neutrality?
Germany to be divided

THE YALTA CONFERENCE
Stalin recognises the "Lublin Committee"
The new government moves in
The conference opens
Roosevelt chosen as Chairman
American vacillation
Formidable negotiator
Churchill's difficult position
The resolutions

Chapter 145 Himmler's Offensive 2269

Himmler's offensive
de Gaulle disapproves
Churchill sides with de Gaulle
The battle for Strasbourg
The German defence
The Colman pocket wiped out
Montgomery and Eisenhower clash again
Support for Eisenhower

Chapter 146 Remagen Bridge 2282

Rundstedt powerless
Allied superiority
Complete surprise
No retreat
Triumphant advance
Surprise crossing

Chapter 147 Across the Rhine 2297

Kesselring caught off balance
To surrender or not?
Scorched earth policy
Montgomery prepares to cross the Rhine
The battle begins
Airborne landings
Large bridgehead
Eisenhower's excellent plan
Collapse of the German 15th Army
The Ruhr pocket
Eisenower gives up the idea of Berlin
Stalin approves warmly
Churchill objects violently
Eisenhower refuses to countermand his orders

Chapter 148 The End in Italy. 2325

Superb defences
Revised plans
The offensive falters
Coriano ridge taken
Winter war
Command shuffles
The last lap

Chapter 149 Germany: The Trap Closes 2353

Montgomery drives for Lubeck
Hamburg and Bremen taken
Canadians in Holland
Last German high command change
More French advances
Patch moves south-east
Berchtesgaden taken

Chapter 150 The Battle of Lake Balaton 2371

The Russian riposte
Vienna falls
The defence of Berlin
Roosevelt dies
The final appeal

Editorial Director: Brian Innes
Editor-in-chief; Brigadier Peter Young, D.S.O., M.C., M.A.
Managing Editor: Richard Humble
Editor: Christopher Chant
Art Editor: Jim Bridge

© Orbis Publishing Limited 1972
© Éditions Alphée, Monaco 1966
Library of Congress Catalog No. 72-95429
Printed in Great Britain

CHAPTER 144
The Allies confer

The QUEBEC Conference

On Tuesday September 6, 1944, Churchill and his three chiefs-of-staff left the Clyde on board the liner *Queen Mary* for Halifax, Nova Scotia. Here a special train took them to Quebec late in the morning of September 11. President Roosevelt and his military colleagues were waiting for the British party. To Winston Churchill's great disappointment Harry Hopkins had excused himself: apart from the health reasons which explained his absence (and these were real enough), he was also suffering the consequences of his loss of favour at the White House at this time.

During this Anglo-American conference, which had been named "Octagon", the discussion concerned mainly the form of participation to be taken by the British forces in the fight against Japan, after the Third Reich had been driven to unconditional surrender. Planning included operations in Burma, a possible air and naval offensive from Australia against Singapore, and putting a Royal Navy formation under the command of the American Pacific Fleet, which had just won a victory at the Marianas Islands and was about to win another at Leyte.

In the European theatre, it was decided not to withdraw a single division from the Allied forces in the Mediterranean until the result of the attack the 15th Army Group was preparing to launch across the Apennines was known; its objective was the Adige line, just short of the Piave.

Occupied Germany

An agreement was also made between the British and the Americans to mark off their future occupation zones in Germany. After some argument about the allocation of the Westphalian industrial basin, it was decided, according to Admiral Leahy, President Roosevelt's Chief-of-Staff, to divide the zones as follows: "(a) The British forces, under a British

▵ *British troops in combat against the Japanese in the Burmese jungle. Operations in this theatre were among the points discussed at Quebec.*
▹ *The highly strategic Burma Road, cutting through the jungle terrain. This was the route by which General Chiang Kai-shek Japanese conquest of Burma in 1942 closed the road, and the Americans subsequently supplied the Chinese by air lift.*

commander, will occupy Germany west of the Rhine and east of the Rhine north of a line from Coblenz following the northern border of Hessen and Nassau to the border of the area allocated to the Soviet Government.

(b) The forces of the United States, under a United States commander, will occupy Germany east of the Rhine, south of the line from Coblenz following the northern border of Hessen–Nassau and west of the area allocated to the Soviet Government.

(c) Control of the ports of Bremen and Bremerhaven and the necessary staging areas in that immediate vicinity will be vested in the commander of the American zone.

(d) American area to have, in addition, access through the western and north-western seaports and passage through the British controlled area.

(e) Accurate delineation of the above outlined British and American areas of control can be made at a later date."

Reading this text one notices that:

1. at this time no French occupation zone was provided for;
2. Bremen and Bremerhaven were included in the American occupation zone because President Roosevelt wanted to make sure that his troops would be supplied without using French territory; and
3. Berlin was not mentioned and there was no reference to the facilities which the two Western powers would require from their Soviet ally if they were to have free access to the German capital at all times.

Robert Murphy, the American diplomat who had just taken up his duties as adviser to General Eisenhower on German affairs, frequently mentioned and deplored this last point. He states in his memoirs that "no provision had been made for the Anglo-American powers to reach that city", and notes that his colleague James Riddleberger, the State Department's delegate to the European Consultative Council in London, who was equally aware of this omission, had suggested that "the occupation zones should converge upon Berlin like slices of pie, thus providing each zone with its own frontage in the capital city". Murphy also asked Riddleberger whom he had approached with his plan. The latter had told Ambassador Winant, who had been opposed to any modification of the original plan and accused Riddleberger of not having confidence in Soviet Russia. Riddleberger replied that on this he was exactly right.

In addition, according to Murphy, the "daydreams" of Winant, the U.S. Ambassador in London, and therefore the American representative for Russo-American affairs at the European Consultative Council, relied too much on Roosevelt's usual formula: "I can handle Stalin."

The Morgenthau Plan

During the "Octagon" Conference the notorious Morgenthau Plan (named after its author, the Secretary of the Treasury), which dealt with the treatment of Germany after its defeat, was endorsed by the British and American Governments.

Since the beginning of August, Eisenhower had been requesting instructions on the attitude to be adopted after the German defeat, and the War Department sent him a note on the subject, asking him to make his observations. However, a member of Eisenhower's staff committed the double indiscretion of getting hold of a copy of this memorandum and sending it to Henry Morgenthau. Morgenthau had wormed his way into the President's favour to such an extent that he was the only member of his cabinet to call him by his first name.

After the cabinet session of August 26, 1944, James V. Forrestal, the Secretary of the Navy, noted in his valuable diary:

"The Secretary of the Treasury (Henry Morgenthau, Jr.) came in with the President with whom he had had lunch. The President said that he had been talking with the Secretary of the Treasury on the general question of the control of Germany after the end of the war. He said that he had just heard about a paper prepared by the Army and that he was not at all satisfied with the severity of the measures proposed. He said that the Germans should have simply a subsistence level of food–as he put it, soup kitchens would be ample to sustain life–that otherwise they should be stripped clean and should not have a level of subsistence above the lowest level of the people they had conquered.

"The Secretary of War (Henry L. Stimson) demurred from this view, but the President continued in the expression of

1

2

3

△ *The principal military participants in the "Octagon" Conference. Discussion here included the part Britain was to play in the war against Japan, and initial agreement was reached over Allied occupation zones in post-war Germany.*

▽ *Henry Morgenthau Jr., U.S. Secretary of the Treasury and author of the Morgenthau Plan for the treatment of Germany after the war. In this, German factories were to be dismantled, mines flooded, raw materials cut off, and the people were to live by subsistence farming. At the conference, Churchill and Roosevelt endorsed this Plan.*

this attitude and finally said he would name a committee composing State, War, and Treasury which would consider the problem of how to handle Germany along the lines that he had outlined, that this committee would consult the Navy whenever naval questions were involved."

According to the plan, Germany would not only have her factories, in particular her steel plants, dismantled, but all her raw material resources also cut off, because she would be permanently forbidden to mine coal and iron ore. Her mines were to be flooded and the German people would have to subsist on crops and cattle-breeding as in the early times of the Holy Roman Empire. Secretary of State Cordell Hull and Secretary of War Henry L. Stimson were firm in their objections, but Roosevelt remained obstinate and, leaving his diplomatic chief in Washington, took Morgenthau with him to the Quebec Conference. It is interesting to note the reception given by Churchill to this inhuman and preposterous project.

Churchill's opinion alters

In the volume of his memoirs entitled *Triumph and Tragedy,* which he wrote in 1953, Churchill tells us:

"At first I violently opposed this idea. But the President, with Mr. Morgenthau – for whom we had much to ask – was so insistent that in the end we agreed to consider it."

This is both true and false. There is no doubt that he recoiled when he learned of the Morgenthau plan, as Lord Moran heard him say on September 13 at the dinner of the Citadel Night, when the subject came up:

"I'm all for disarming Germany, but we ought not to prevent her living decently. There are bonds between the working classes of all countries, and the English people will not stand for the policy you are advocating." And he is said to have muttered: "You cannot indict a whole nation."

On the other hand, when Roosevelt and Morgenthau insisted, Churchill, in spite of what he said, not only promised them that he would examine the plan for reducing Germany to a pastoral existence, but after it had been examined by Professor Lindemann (later Lord Cherwell), put his signature to it on September 15. According to Lord Moran, Cherwell as Churchill's scientific adviser had persuaded the Prime Minister, explaining what he had not noticed at first sight, that "the plan will save Britain from bankruptcy by eliminating a dangerous competitor".

4

5

6

1. General H. H. Arnold
2. Air Chief-Marshal Sir Charles Portal
3. General Sir Alan Brooke
4. Field-Marshal Sir John Dill
5. Admiral E. J. King
6. General G. C. Marshall
7. Admiral of the Fleet Sir Dudley Pound
8. Admiral W. D. Leahy

It is tempting to dismiss the versions of Churchill and his doctor out of hand, as they are contradictory. However, the evidence given by Anthony Eden, now Lord Avon, supports Lord Moran's version point by point; he writes:

"On the morning of September 15th I joined the Prime Minister and the President, who were by now in agreement in their approval of the plan. Cherwell had supported Morgenthau and their joint advocacy had prevailed. Large areas of the Ruhr and the Saar were to be stripped of their manufacturing industries and turned into agricultural lands. It was as if one were to take the Black Country and turn it into Devonshire. I did not like the plan, nor was I convinced that it was to our national advantage.

"I said so, and also suggested that Mr. Cordell Hull's opinion should be sought for. This was the only occasion I can remember when the Prime Minister showed impatience with my views before foreign representatives. He resented my criticism of something which he and the President had approved, not I am sure on his account, but on the President's."

Meanwhile, Cordell Hull, on whose territory Morgenthau was trespassing, and Stimson, who refused to admit defeat, were left behind in Washington. However, they did not relax their opposition to the Morgenthau plan and on September 18, the deputy Secretary of War, John McCloy, also condemned it to Forrestal:

"In general the programme according to Mr. McCloy, called for the conscious destruction of the economy in Germany and the encouragement of a state of impoverishment and disorder. He said he felt the Army's role in any programme would be most difficult because the Army, by training and instinct, would naturally turn to the re-creation of order as soon as possible, whereas under this programme they apparently were to encourage the opposite."

7

Eisenhower's view: "silly and criminal"

McCloy was not exaggerating in interpreting the feeling of the U.S. high command as he did. Already in August, when Morgenthau had visited S.H.A.E.F., Eisenhower had told him that "it would be madness" to deprive the Germans of their natural resources and he rejected all arguments to the contrary. In *Crusade in Europe* Eisenhower bluntly describes his attitude:

"I emphatically repudiated one suggestion I had heard that the Ruhr mines should be flooded. This seemed silly and

8

△ President Franklin Roosevelt reviews a guard of honour at the Quebec Conference, September 1944.

criminal to me . . . These views were presented to everyone who queried me on the subject, both then and later. They were eventually placed before the President and the Secretary of State when they came to Potsdam in July 1945."

Harry Hopkins himself joined this protest; Roosevelt and Morgenthau therefore had to shelve indefinitely the plan so accurately described by General Eisenhower. Moreover in London, the Treasury informed the Prime Minister that if German productivity were completely destroyed, she would no longer be able to pay for her imports, and England would therefore lose an important market as soon as peace came. The argument with which Morgenthau had won over Lord Cherwell was therefore entirely refuted. In these circumstances, Churchill made no bones about going back on his agreement, and was quite ready, when he wrote the penultimate volume of his war memoirs, to forget that he had given it, even in writing: he had in fact contributed to drawing up the resolution that had been formulated. The Morgenthau plan was a dead letter.

German propaganda benefits

However, the Morgenthau plan had certain consequences, even though it had been abandoned by the Western Allies. What was learned of it in Germany gave Goebbels a propaganda line which he developed on the radio with his usual diabolical skill. The Allies, he pointed out to his fellow countrymen on every possible occasion, were not only making war against the Nazis, but against the whole German people, who would be condemned to the bleakest poverty by a ruthless enemy if they were so naïve as to cease their resistance and disown their Führer; in destructive purpose, Anglo-Saxon "Jewry" was no different from the Moscow Bolsheviks. The Quebec resolution, moreover, demonstrated the error of people who, like the July 20 conspirators, thought they could spare the German people the Soviet invasion by paying for it at the price of capitulation to the West.

"Que diable allait-il faire dans cette galère?" (What on earth was he doing in this company?) One might well echo Molière's question when considering the visit Churchill made to Moscow from October 9 to 16, 1944.

According to Churchill's own account, the Soviet penetration into south-east Europe compelled him to make this journey. With Rumania's about-face, followed by the Bulgarian armistice, the launching of the Soviet autumn offensive, and "in spite of the Warsaw tragedy . . . I felt the need of another personal meeting with Stalin . . . As the victory of the Grand Alliance became only a matter of time it was natural that Russian ambitions should grow. Communism raised its head behind the thundering Russian battle-front. Russia was the Deliverer, and Communism the gospel she brought."

At this juncture, neither Bulgaria's nor Rumania's fates were of the slightest concern to Great Britain; on the other hand Churchill was very worried about what would happen to Poland and Greece. Great Britain considered herself responsible for the restoration of their governments-in-exile, if this was what their peoples really wished. And it was essential that they should be able to express themselves freely. In fact, this was far from certain since Stalin had set up a Polish government subservient to him in Lublin, and George Papandreou's Greek Government seemed to be dependent on the Communist resistance group.

On the other hand, work was not proceeding well at Dumbarton Oaks, where an inter-Allied conference was meeting for the purpose of laying the foundations of a future United Nations Organisation. The Russians clashed with the British and Americans both on the composition of the General Assembly and on the balloting method for the Security Council. Moscow was now determined that the rule of Great Power unanimity should prevail. Once again, according to Churchill in 1953, he felt he should strike while the iron was hot:

"I felt sure we could only reach good

▵ *Lord Moran, Churchill's ever-present physician. He saw Churchill every day and was able to note his reaction to events as they happened. His book* Churchill: The Struggle for Survival *thus provides valuable insight into Churchill's thoughts, especially with regard to his attitude towards the Morgenthau Plan and the settlement of the Polish question.*

decisions with Russia while we had the comradeship of a common foe as a bond. Hitler and Hitlerism were doomed; but after Hitler what?"

Churchill's initiative

Therefore Churchill took the initiative in a telegram on September 27, and proposed a visit to the Kremlin. Stalin, in his reply of September 30, welcomed the idea "warmly". Roosevelt excused himself from accompanying Churchill to Moscow as the presidential elections were imminent, and his absence from the U.S.A. at this time might well have prejudiced the result to his disadvantage. However, his ambassador in the U.S.S.R., Averell Harriman, was to replace him, taking part in the conversations as an observer, and as Roosevelt's message of October 4 stated:

"While naturally Averell will not be in a position to commit the United States – I could not permit anyone to commit me in advance – he will be able to keep me informed, and I have told him to return and report to me as soon as the conference is over."

And as he feared that his British partner might indulge in some passing whim, Roosevelt sent word to Stalin on the same day:

"I am sure you understand that in this global war there is literally no question, military or political, in which the United States is not interested. I am firmly convinced that the three of us, and only the three of us, can find the solution of the questions still unresolved. In this sense, while appreciating Mr. Churchill's desire for the meeting, I prefer to regard your forthcoming talks with the Prime Minister as preliminary to a meeting of the three of us which can take place any time after the elections here as far as I am concerned."

Churchill does not mention it in his memoirs, but he took great offence at the President's precaution, according to Lord Moran, who in his capacity as Churchill's doctor saw him every day. But what was more serious, according to Moran, by the end of September "the advance of the Red Army has taken possession of [Churchill's] mind. Once they got into a country, it would not be easy to get them out. Our army in Italy was too weak to keep them in check. He might get his way with Stalin by other means.

"All might be well if he could win Stalin's friendship. After all it was stupid of the President to suppose that he was the only person who could manage Stalin. Winston told me that he had found he could talk to Stalin as one human being to another. Stalin, he was sure, would be sensible. He went on to speak of this proffer of friendship to Stalin as if it were an ingenious idea that had just occurred to him, and while he spoke his eyes popped and his words tumbled over each other in his excitement. He could think of nothing else. It had ceased to be a means to an end; it had become an end in itself. He sat up in bed.

"'If we three come together,' he said, 'everything is possible – absolutely anything.'"

As can be seen, there is a strong difference between Churchill's attitude in his memoirs and his reactions at the time as his doctor saw them; in 1953, when the cold war was at its height and he had just been re-elected, Churchill could not admit to his readers that he had deluded himself into thinking he could win Stalin over.

Spheres of influence

Accompanied by Anthony Eden, General Sir Hastings Ismay, his chief-of-staff, and Field-Marshal Sir Alan Brooke, the C.I.G.S., the Prime Minister travelled via Naples, Cairo, and Simferopol' and arrived in Moscow on the evening of October 9. At 2200 hours, he and Eden were conducted to Stalin's office. Stalin, accompanied by Molotov, was waiting for him. And in the absence of Averell Harriman, the four men lost no time in making a preliminary survey of the world situation.

Doubtless Harriman would not have objected to their decision to invite the Polish government to send a delegation to Moscow. But perhaps he would have thought that Churchill was unduly compromising the future as well as the U.S.A. if he had heard him tell Stalin:

"Let us settle about our affairs in the Balkans. Your armies are in Roumania and Bulgaria. We have interests, missions, and agents there. Don't let us get at cross-purposes in small ways. So far as Britain and Russia are concerned, how would it do for you to have ninety

per cent predominance in Roumania, for us to have ninety per cent of the say in Greece, and go fifty-fifty about Yugoslavia?"

And even more so if he had seen Churchill make in writing a proposal which had never been agreed by London and Washington. Churchill in fact, whilst his words were being translated, scribbled on a half sheet of paper:

"Roumania
Russia 90%
The others 10%
Greece
Great Britain 90%
(in accord with U.S.A.)

△△ *The "Red Orchestra" batters Nazi ears with its successes in Poland and East Prussia.*
△◁ *How* Simplicissimus *saw "free" Polish broadcasts from the "Soviet paradise".*
△ *John Bull tells Poland "The best solution is to give him all he steals and you'll be friends."*

▲ *George Papandreou, Greek Prime Minister. In April 1944, he was brought out of Greece by the Allies to form a Greek government-in-exile in Cairo. Churchill was concerned about the fate of Greece after the war and considered Great Britain responsible for the restoration of the government-in-exile. When the Germans withdrew from Greece in October 1944, Papandreou returned to Athens as Prime Minister.*

▷ *Churchill arrives in Moscow, October 9, 1944. Concerned by the increasing Soviet penetration of south-east Europe, Churchill initiated this conference himself, determined to reach amicable agreement with Stalin over the future of the Balkans and, more important, Poland.*

Russia	10%
Yugoslavia	50-50%
Hungary	50-50%
Bulgaria	
Russia	75%
The others	25%"

Stalin ticked the paper passed to him by Churchill, who writes: "It was all settled in no more time than it takes to set down."

In his memoirs, Churchill assures us it was only valid for the duration of the war and that it did not prejudice solutions which would be kept for the future peace conference. But if we accept this version, it is hard to understand the irritation with which he writes a few lines later:

"'Might it not be thought rather cynical if it seemed we had disposed of these issues, so fateful to millions of people, in such an offhand manner? Let us burn the paper.' 'No, you keep it,' said Stalin."

In exchange for a half-sheet of paper

the Western Powers, on Churchill's initiative, had abdicated all influence in Bucharest and Sofia, and implicitly left the Rumanians and Bulgarians to face the Soviet giant alone.

In addition, it was later observed that this arrangement on October 9 did not remove the threat of Communist subversion from Greece, in spite of the percentage of that unhappy country conceded to Great Britain by the Kremlin.

Tito goes it alone

The 50 per cent influence allotted to Britain in Yugoslavia dropped to zero even before hostilities ended in Europe, and Tito tore up the agreement he had concluded in the previous year with Dr. Subašić, Prime Minister of the Yugoslav government-in-exile. Obviously, in October 1944, Churchill and Eden no longer had any illusions about the future direction of Marshal Tito's policy, in spite of the Anglo-American arms deliveries which had saved him from defeat and death. Moreover, in this division of spheres of influence, it was clear that Churchill had completely forgotten Albania, on which Greece had some claims.

Eden *versus* Molotov

But before 24 hours had passed, Molotov tried to obtain from Eden some modifications of the percentages agreed on the day before. He received a curt refusal, but a note of Eden's shows that his own report of the incident was coolly received by the Prime Minister, who was wrapped up in his own illusions:

"W. rather upset by my report. I think he thought I had dispelled good atmosphere he had created night before. But I explained this was the real battle and I could not and would not give way."

His firmness was rewarded, as Molotov undertook to call on the Bulgarians to evacuate immediately the Greek and Yugoslav provinces which they had occupied by German agreement in April and May 1941. As regards Yugoslavia, Eden wrote:

"We also spoke of Yugoslavia, when Stalin said that Tito thought the Croats and Slovenes would refuse to join in any government under King Peter. He himself had the impression that the King was ineffective. I replied that I was sure the King had courage and I thought that he had intelligence. Mr. Churchill interjected that the King was very young.

"'How old is he?' asked Stalin. 'Twenty-one,' I answered. 'Twenty-one!' exclaimed Stalin with a burst of pride, 'Peter the Great was ruler of Russia at seventeen.' For that moment, at least, Stalin was more nationalist than communist, the same mood as had seen the disappearance for the time being of the portraits of Marx and Engels from the Kremlin rooms and their replacement by Kutuzov and Suvorov."

Poles in exile

On October 13, the Polish delegation of the government-in-exile, consisting of its Prime Minister, Stanislas Mikolajczyk, Professor Grabski, and Foreign Minister Tadeusz Romer started discussions with Stalin, Molotov, Churchill, Eden, and Harriman, who had been instructed to keep strictly to his rôle as observer. They intended to reach an agreement on two questions: firstly, the eastern frontiers of Poland; and secondly, the formation of a unified Polish government, including the London government's representatives and members of the Lublin "National Committee". Although they expected to make some territorial sacrifices to the Soviet Union, Mikolajczyk and his colleagues were aghast when they discovered that the Teheran agreement (which had been concluded behind their backs by the "Big Three") had prescribed the Curzon Line as their country's frontier; thus 48 per cent of Polish territory would be surrendered to the U.S.S.R. without the population involved being consulted about the transfer.

The Polish prime minister's protests against the acquiescence which was being demanded of him left Stalin cold and uncompromising.

After this session, the British and Poles met. Churchill lost his temper and started threatening the unfortunate Mikolajczyk:

"I pressed Mikolajczyk hard to consider two things, namely, *de facto* acceptance of the Curzon Line, with interchange of population, and a friendly discussion with the Lublin Polish Committee so that a united Poland might be established."

△ *Averell Harriman* (right), *U.S. Ambassador in Moscow, with Anthony Eden, who accompanied Churchill to the Moscow Conference. Harriman represented Roosevelt at the conference, but was absent when Stalin and Churchill decided on spheres of influence in the Balkans.*

BALANCE OF POWER
ATLANTIK CHARTA

This is the version of the meeting in Churchill's memoirs, but it seems to be a typically British understatement. In fact, on the next day the Prime Minister confided to Moran: "I was pretty rough with Mikolajczyk . . . He was obstinate and I lost my temper." A few hours later Churchill returned to the subject: "I shook my fist at him and lost my temper."

It is hard to accept Mikolajczyk's account of the conversation; his memoirs were published in New York and Toronto and were not challenged by Churchill. The striking thing about Churchill's diatribes, as recounted by Mikolajczyk, is not so much their violence ("You're not a government! You're an unreasonable people who want to shipwreck Europe. I'll leave you to stew in your own juice. You have no sense of responsibility when you want to abandon the people in your care, and you've no idea of their sufferings. You've no thought for anything but your own wretched, mean, and egotistical interests.") and their threats ("We shall not part as friends. I shall tell the world how unreasonable you've shown yourselves to be . . . We'll take a stand and break away from you if you continue to prevaricate. I'll consider opening relations with the other Poles. The Lublin government can work perfectly. They'll be the government for sure.") as his confidence that if the Polish Government gave in to the Big Three, all would be for the best in the best of all possible Europes. Churchill continued:

"Our relations with Russia are better than they've ever been. I expect them to remain so . . . we do not intend to jeopardise the peace of Europe . . . Your discussions are nothing more than criminal attempts to undermine goodwill between the Allies with your *Liberum veto*. It is a criminal act of your doing!"

Assuming this determinedly optimistic point of view, Churchill described to Mikolajczyk the advantage which would compensate Poland for the sacrifices he was calling upon her to make:

"But think what you will get in exchange. You will have a country. I will see that a British ambassador is sent to you. And there will also be an ambassador from the United States, the greatest military power in the world . . .

"If you accept the Curzon line, the United States will devote themselves most actively to the reconstruction of Poland and will doubtless give you large loans, perhaps even without your having to ask for them. We will help you too, but we will be poor after this war. You are *obliged* to accept the decision of the great powers."

Mikolajczyk, in spite of Churchill's tone of voice, was not completely insensitive to this argument. He proposed a compromise, in which he was prepared to recognise the Curzon Line as Poland's eastern frontier, provided that the Drohobycz and Boryslaw oil wells, as well as the great historically and traditionally Polish cities of L'vov and Vilnyus on the east of the line, remained Polish. But Stalin refused to countenance any such concessions.

Combined Polish government?

In doing this, Stalin was risking nothing; on the one hand his armies had crossed the Curzon Line on the entire front between the Niemen and the Carpathians; on the other hand, the Lublin Committee delegates, Osóbka-Morawski and Bierut, stated in the presence of Churchill, Eden, and Harriman:

"'We are here to demand on behalf of Poland that Lvov shall belong to Russia. That is the will of the Polish people.'

"When this had been translated from Polish into English and Russian I looked at Stalin and saw an understanding twinkle in his expressive eyes, as much as to say, 'What about that for our Soviet teaching!'"

In their memoirs Churchill and Eden made no attempt to conceal their disgust when they heard these servile commonplaces. Nevertheless Mikolajczyk received the peremptory advice to accept these foreign agents in his government. Otherwise it would be the end of Poland.

Conduct of the war

As Roosevelt had wished, the problems relating to the articles of the future international organisation were not mentioned during the conference. The agenda was devoted to presenting, discussing, and putting final touches to the plans for the last phase of the war in Europe and for the participation of the Red Army in the war against Japan.

△ *Marshal Josep Broz "Tito", Yugoslav Communist Party chief and leader of the partisan resistance movement. Tito won British support and aid in 1943, and by August 1944 the Germans were retreating before the partisans. The future of Yugoslavia was discussed at Moscow, but Tito refused to countenance the restoration of King Peter. In March 1945, he set up a provisional government with himself as Prime Minister.*

△ ◁◁ *"And look! The nice uncle is even offering you a stool."*

△ ◁ *The imbalance of power by late on in the war.*

▽ ◁ *Poland's pathetic plight: "And we all put our faith in this boat."*

With his usual clarity, Brooke set out the situation on the Western Front and in Italy, and explained General Eisenhower's intentions. The deputy chief-of-staff of the Red Army, General Antonov, then spoke, and Brooke noted in his diary that he was extremely pleased with the ensuing discussion.

On October 15, the war against Japan was discussed, with particular reference to the Red Army and the possibility of moving supplies via the trans-Siberian railway for an offensive in Manchuria with 60 divisions and appropriate air forces. Stalin took over from his military colleague and explained the difficulties of the project. According to Brooke:

"He displayed an astounding knowledge of technical railway details, had read past history of fighting in that theatre and from this knowledge drew very sound deductions. I was more than ever impressed by his military ability."

△ Bierut, President of the Lublin "Committee of National Liberation". Churchill thought the Lublin Poles were "mere pawns of Russia" when he met them at the Moscow Conference.
▷ The Communist provisional government of Poland at a march-past in Lublin. The officers are saluting in the traditional Polish manner, with three fingers (one for the Father, one for the Son, and one for the Holy Ghost) despite their new Communist persuasion.
△▷ Roosevelt, on board the cruiser Quincy *travelling to the Yalta Conference, stops off in the Great Bitter Lakes to entertain King Farouk of Egypt on his birthday. This delighted Farouk, who had felt slighted by other Allied leaders.*
▽▷ London, Washington, and Moscow recognised General de Gaulle's provisional government as the government of the French Republic at the Moscow Conference. Here, General de Gaulle is seen arriving at Moscow. He was not, however, invited to the Yalta and Potsdam Conferences.

Violate Swiss neutrality?

Complete military agreement was reached by the Big Three; Stalin, however, made one suggestion that was rejected by Churchill, although he does not mention it in his memoirs. On the other hand, Admiral Leahy wrote:

"Harriman reported on October 13 that Stalin advocated only a holding effort in North Italy, coupled with an advance toward Vienna from the head of the Adriatic Sea. The Soviet chieftain also advocated an advance through Switzerland to get into the rear of the Siegfried Line fortifications. The latter suggestion certainly did not place much value on the Allied claim that the sovereignty of small states must not be violated."

In June 1966, Harriman's despatch concerning this suggestion was published by the State Department, together with the diplomatic documents of the time. We can therefore make the following correction to Leahy's statement. Stalin did not advise his Western Allies to pursue their attack in northern Italy but, noting that the Germans were resisting them strongly in the Apennines and on the Siegfried Line, he suggested that they should withdraw ten of the 25 divisions which were in the line between the Adriatic and the Tyrrhenian Sea. These divisions would invade Switzerland, turn the German defences north of Basle and attempt to co-ordinate its operations with the Red Army's in Austria. Switzerland, he stated, had played a double game during the war and must be compelled by force of arms to give the Allies access to her territory.

Churchill, according to Harriman's report, opposed this plan energetically, not only because it was militarily impracticable, which was true, but even more because it was contrary to the Western Allies' political principles. Stalin did not persist with the idea. Churchill, however, was so impressed by the bitterly hostile way Stalin spoke about Switzerland that on December 3 he dictated the following note to Eden:

"I put this down for record. Of all the neutrals Switzerland has the greatest right to distinction. She has been the sole international force linking the hideously sundered nations and ourselves. What does it matter whether she has been able to give us the commercial advantages we desire or has given too many to the Germans, to keep herself alive? She has been a democratic State, standing for freedom in self-defence among her mountains, and in thought, in spite of race, largely on our side.

"I was astonished at U.J.'s [Uncle Joe,

Churchill's and Roosevelt's name for Stalin] savageness against her, and, much though I respect that great and good man, I was entirely uninfluenced by his attitude. He called them 'swine', and does not use that sort of language without meaning it. I am sure we ought to stand by Switzerland, and we ought to explain to U.J. why it is we do so. The moment for sending such a message should be carefully chosen . . ."

He also, via secret channels, alerted the Swiss Federal Council, which received the warning gratefully.

Germany to be divided

Churchill and Stalin decided that Germany would be divided up and that a southern state, consisting of Baden, Württemberg, Bavaria, and Austria, would be formed. To give more stability to this Danubian confederation, Churchill wanted Hungary to join it, but Stalin, who had designs on Hungary, refused.

The only success claimed by the British Government was the *de jure* recognition by London, Washington, and Moscow of General de Gaulle's provisional government as the government of France.

Much has been written, at any rate in the West, about the "Argonaut" Conference, during which Roosevelt, Churchill, Stalin, and their chief political and military colleagues met at Yalta in the Crimea. In 1955, the State Department published a wide collection of diplomatic documents relating to the Big Three's meeting, the discussions they had together, and the resolutions and agreements they signed. Thus we can compare these authentic records with the statements of those taking part in the conference.

During the period between Churchill's Moscow journey and the Yalta conference, a number of occurrences which influenced the course of negotiations should be mentioned.

On November 7, 1944, the American people re-elected Roosevelt to a fourth term as President, admittedly by about 3,000,000 fewer votes than in 1940. Obviously, in making his choice, the American voter was relying on the adage that one should not change horses in mid-course. Nevertheless, the victor of this exhausting campaign had neglected his brief and, in addition, he was in a very poor state of health.

"The President looked old and thin and drawn; he had a cape or shawl over his shoulders and appeared shrunken; he sat looking straight ahead with his mouth open, as if he were not taking things in." This was Moran's description of him on February 3, and the next day he wrote:

"It was not only his physical deterioration that had caught their attention. He intervened very little in the discussions, sitting with his mouth open. If he has sometimes been short of facts about the subject under discussion his shrewdness has covered this up. Now, they say, the shrewdness has gone, and there is nothing left." Again, Moran noted on the 7th:

"To a doctor's eye, the President appears a very sick man. He has all the symptoms of hardening of the arteries of the brain in an advanced stage, so that I give him only a few months to live."

For personal reasons Roosevelt, before

◁ *The splendid Livadia Palace, where the Yalta Conference was held to decide the fate of the world.*

Δ *Molotov signs the Franco-Russian pact, watched by de Gaulle and Stalin. But by the time of the Yalta Conference relations were not so amicable.*

starting on his electoral campaign, had dropped his previous Vice-President, Henry A. Wallace, in favour of Harry S. Truman, the senator from Missouri. This was a stroke of luck for the free world. Truman, a man of strong character, was, however, quite unprepared for his task when on April 12, 1945 he was suddenly called upon to take over the responsibilities of power.

Moreover the Secretary of State, Cordell Hull, had now reached retirement age. Roosevelt appointed Edward R. Stettinius in his place. Stettinius was a conscientious civil servant who knew his job thoroughly, but he was called upon to take over his duties under a President in very poor health, to say the least, and was faced by an opposite number as redoubtable and experienced in international affairs as Molotov.

Stalin recognises the "Lublin Committee"

Mikolajczyk, when he returned to London, found that the majority of his government disapproved of the concessions he had felt compelled to make to the U.S.S.R. He therefore accepted the consequences, and resigned. He was succeeded by Tomasz Arciszewski, a militant social-democrat. But although he was more to the left than his predecessor, the new head of the exile government failed to move the Kremlin.

When he resigned on November 24, 1944, Mikolajczyk handed over two documents concerning the policy of the U.S.A. and Great Britain towards the future Polish state. In a letter after he had been re-elected, President Roosevelt defined the American attitude clearly and positively:

"The Government of the United States is, most determinedly, in favour of a strong Polish state, free, independent, and conscious of the rights of the Polish people, to run its internal politics as it sees fit, without any outside interference."

Certainly the U.S.A. could not depart from their traditional policy and guarantee the frontiers of the future Polish state, but they were ready to play a very large part in its economic reconstruction.

Moreover, on the previous November 2, on Churchill's instructions, Sir Alexander Cadogan, Permanent Under-Secretary of State at the Foreign Office, wrote to Romer, the Polish Foreign Minister, a letter of which the following is an extract:

"Finally you ask if His Majesty's Government will guarantee the independence and integrity of the new Polish state. On this point the reply of His Majesty's Government is that they are ready to give this guarantee conjointly with the Soviet Government. If the Government of the United States also believed that it could associate itself in this guarantee, that would be so much the better, but His Majesty's Government does not make this a condition of the guarantee, which it is ready to give conjointly with that of the Soviet Government."

It is evident that Great Britain's attitude in this declaration fell considerably short of the U.S.A.'s, as she made her guarantee of Polish independence subject to an agreement with the Soviet Union. What would happen if Stalin refused this guarantee?

On December 18, a statement by Secretary of State Stettinius, recalling the terms of Roosevelt's letter to Mikolajczyk, was brought to Stalin's notice. On December 27, Stalin in his reply to Roosevelt maintained that this statement had been overtaken by events; then after a long diatribe against Arciszewski and his colleagues, he added in so many words:

"I must say frankly that in the event of the Polish Committee of National Liberation becoming a Provisional Polish Government, the Soviet Government will, in view of the foregoing, have no serious reasons for postponing its recognition."

Then, in spite of a letter from Roosevelt, who said he was "disturbed and deeply disappointed" by this declaration and by the hasty Moscow decision, he proceeded to recognise the Lublin Committee on January 5, 1945; he gave Roosevelt the following explanation:

"Of course I quite understand your proposal for postponing recognition of the Provisional Government of Poland by the Soviet Union for a month. But one circumstance makes me powerless to comply with your wish. The point is that on December 27 the Presidium of the Supreme Soviet of the U.S.S.R., replying to the corresponding question by the Poles, declared that it would recognise the Provisional Government of Poland the moment it was set up. This circumstance makes me powerless to comply with your wish."

1

2

3

4

5

But he omitted to say that he had dictated this request for recognition to the "Polish Committee of National Liberation."

The new government moves in

It was in this sort of atmosphere that the Yalta Conference opened. Certainly Roosevelt had no intention of recognising the puppet government which Stalin controlled, and Churchill even less so. But in the meantime events had moved on. In fact just when the three delegations were holding their first session, Zhukov's advance guard reached the bend of the Oder whilst Konev's was about to take Breslau. Except for the Polish corridor, all Polish territory was in the hands of the Russians, who were everywhere setting up the Lublin Committee's representatives and hunting down the partisans who had been fighting the Germans for five years under the command of the Polish government-in-exile.

The conference opens

On February 2, Roosevelt, who had arrived on the cruiser *Quincy,* and Churchill, who had flown in, met at Valletta in Malta. They joined the Combined Chiefs-of-Staff Committee, which had been in session for three days and was completing plans for the great operation to take the British and the Americans into the centre of Germany. Then the two delegations flew to the Crimea and on the evening of February 3 moved into the buildings reserved for them: the Americans into the former imperial palace of Livadia; the British five miles away in

1. *Harry Hopkins*
2. *Alger Hiss*
3. *James V. Forrestal*
4. *Robert Winant*
5. *Edward R. Stettinius*

Harry S. Truman was born in 1884. He was a Senator for Missouri when the United States entered the war, and soon entered the limelight as chairman of the Senate Special Commission looking into the National Defense Program. Truman headed the committee with tact and care, and saved the U.S. billions of dollars by pruning costs in the allocation of contracts. His success in this was instrumental in his selection by Roosevelt as Vice-Presidential running mate in the 1944 election campaign. When Roosevelt died on April 12, 1945, Truman became President. Because he had not been in his predecessor's inner circle, Truman had at first to rely on Roosevelt's cabinet in following up the policies already in operation. But as 1945 progressed, he gradually phased out Roosevelt's appointees in favour of his own. He continued to follow the general line of Roosevelt's policies, however, and pressed on with preparations for the San Francisco Conference, which was to set up the United Nations Organisation. Unlike Roosevelt, however, he soon saw what Stalin's real intentions towards Europe were, and that there was little the Western Allies could do about it. Truman attended the Potsdam Conference in July 1945, and authorised the atom bombing of Hiroshima and Nagasaki.

the Vorontzov villa. Stalin and his colleagues were to stay at the Yusupov Palace halfway between them, an arrangement obviously calculated to prevent any Anglo-American private conversations and to make *tête-à-tête* talks with Roosevelt easier.

The first such meeting took place in the afternoon of February 4, and the President was moved to get Stalin to repeat his Teheran toast (that 50,000 German officers should be shot) because Roosevelt maintained the devastation caused by the Wehrmacht in the Crimea gave him a desire for revenge.

Roosevelt chosen as chairman

A few hours later the conference opened in the Livadia Palace, and Stalin immediately proposed that there should be no rotation of chairmanship, but that Roosevelt should chair the proceedings for the whole meeting.

Arthur Conte, in his *Yalta ou le partage du monde,* has noted that this was a skilful Soviet manoeuvre, as it was not intended

▵ ◃ *The Combined Chiefs-of-Staff Committee in session in Malta, January-February 1944, completing plans for the advance into central Germany. Roosevelt and Churchill joined the committee briefly before continuing their journey to Yalta.*
▿ ◃ ◃ *Reunion on board the cruiser* Quincy, *at anchor off Malta: Roosevelt, General Marshall (on the right), Vice-Admiral Cooke (on the left), and Admiral King (back view).*
▿ ◃ *Churchill and Roosevelt acknowledge their reception at Yalta. Molotov is on Churchill's right. Note how ill Roosevelt looks; Lord Moran said at the time that he appeared "shrunken".*
▵ *Russia sits down to a nourishing bowl of "little states of Europe" soup, with the comment "You can see how happy I am to swallow up the people you abandoned and I freed." In the pot in this German cartoon are Lithuania, Finland, and Holland.*

merely as a practical working arrangement: "This also showed a remarkable appreciation of Roosevelt's psychology, by strengthening him in the awareness of his superiority. He was also dissociating himself from British imperialism. It in fact separated the British and the Americans by conferring the chairmanship on the American; Roosevelt thus had power to arbitrate, a conciliatory rôle which would naturally lead him to show increased understanding of the Russian position. Stalin immediately gave himself a big advantage while appearing to give it to Roosevelt."

American vacillation

Eden also noted that the American president was "vague and loose and ineffective", letting the discussion drift on, without being able to pin Stalin and Churchill down to firm and precise terms. The various questions on the agenda were discussed unmethodically, by fits and starts, and Harry Hopkins several times had to bring the discussion back to the subject by passing notes to Roosevelt. But the bias of these notes can easily be guessed, as in spite of the troublesome state of his health, the so-called *éminence grise* of the White House was still strongly pro-Soviet.

Secretary of State Stettinius was too new in his job to know how to assert himself usefully in the discussion. As for the fourth member of the American delegation, the diplomat Alger Hiss, whose particular responsibility was questions relating to the future United Nations Organisation, he was later condemned to five years' imprisonment on January 22, 1950 by a New York court for perjury about his Communist associations.

Another circumstance played against the two Western powers; this was the ten day period allowed by the American constitution to the President to approve or veto bills adopted by the Congress. As he could not do this by cable or radio, it was essential for him not to prolong his stay in the Crimea beyond a week. Stalin, however, was in no hurry and was ready to sell Roosevelt time in exchange for concessions.

Formidable negotiator

Since he had seen Stalin at work, Anthony Eden refers to his diplomatic talents in a way that reminds one of Field-Marshal Sir Alan Brooke's references to his strategic abilities:

"Marshal Stalin as a negotiator was the toughest proposition of all. Indeed, after something like thirty years' experience of international conferences of one kind and another, if I had to pick a team for going into a conference room, Stalin would be my first choice. Of course the man was ruthless and of course he knew his purpose. He never wasted a word. He never stormed, he was

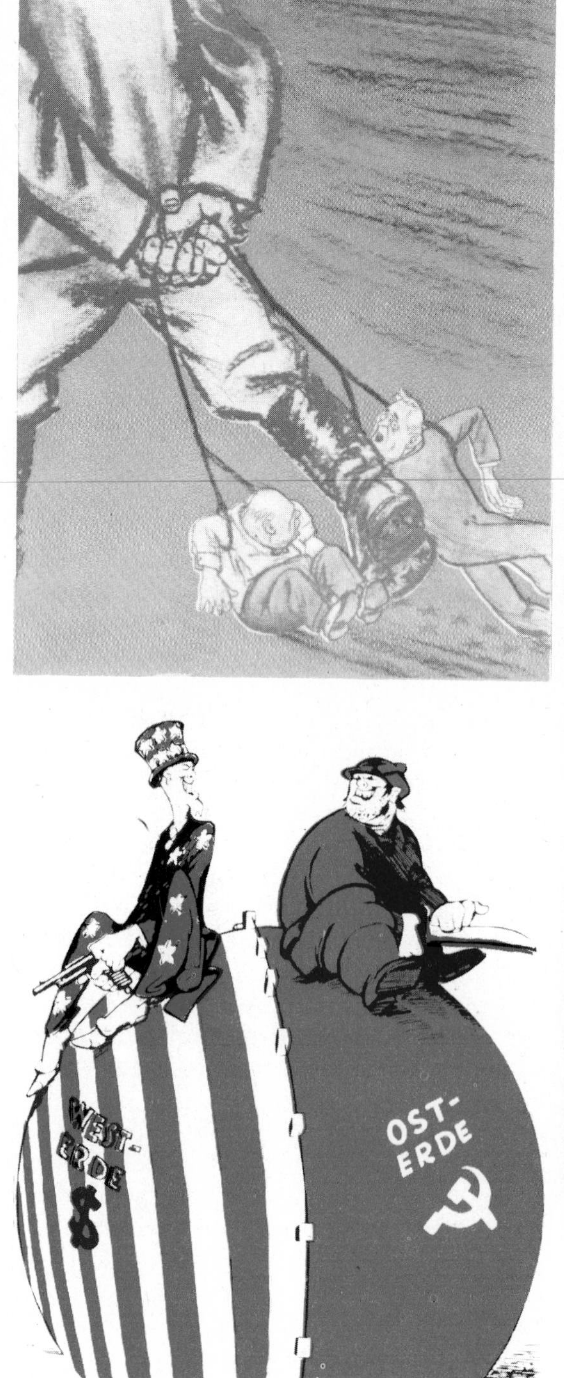

Three German comments on Allied relations:
△ Stalin, past master of the shot-in-the-neck method of execution, sets the table for the next conference with his latest invention.
△▷ "I have the feeling, my dear Roosevelt, that we've been left decidedly behind the marshal," says Churchill.
▷ Overheard during the post-war carve-up of the world: "Well, Sam, what are you doing?" "I was just thinking how I could repay you for your great help." "Incredible! I was just thinking the same thing."

seldom even irritated. Hooded, calm, never raising his voice, he avoided the repeated negatives of Molotov which were so exasperating to listen to. By more subtle methods he got what he wanted without having seemed so obdurate."

Nevertheless, Eden also acknowledged that Molotov was a first-rate assistant to Stalin. One may well suppose that when responsibilities were assigned, the orders given to Molotov were to adopt such a harsh tone that when Stalin took over negotiations in the style so vividly described by Eden, the British and American representatives (in particular Roosevelt, Stettinius, and James) could tell one another gratefully: "After the rain comes the sun."

Churchill's difficult position

Under these circumstances it is not hard to see that the British delegation had no easy task, faced with the vacillations of American policy and Stalin's firm resolve to make the maximum possible advances in all parts of the world. Thus the British did not receive the immediate support of their natural allies when they proposed the immediate and simultaneous evacuation of Persia by the British and Soviet forces that had occupied the country since August 1941. Similarly, the Soviet Union succeeded in imposing its attitude about a revision, once peace came, of the

◁ *The three delegations get down to work. Stalin is seated second from left at the top, Roosevelt at the right, and Churchill at bottom left, with a cigar.*
△ *Death comments "But why argue about future supplies of cannon fodder, my dear sirs? I'm quite content with your present ones."*
▽ ◁ *Eden comments on his Russian opposite number: "Molotov clearly isn't a devious character. His territorial ambitions aren't difficult to see."*

Montreux Convention. This had, since July 20, 1936, laid down the law concerning the control of the Turkish narrows. Russia was thus in a position to start a very unpleasant quarrel with Turkey until President Truman intervened and restored order.

Therefore Churchill left the Crimea full of forebodings, quite the reverse of his happy mood of the previous October 9, when he landed at Moscow airport. But to the last day of his life he did his best to deny any responsibility for the inexorable process which led to the enslavement of 120 million Europeans behind the Iron Curtain. According to Churchill, everything was decided at Yalta during the conference when he was, if one can put it like that, "sandwiched" between Stalin and Roosevelt. In this way he was able to divest himself of his responsibility

in this most unjust settlement of World War II, making Roosevelt shoulder it all. But in view of the documents just quoted, it is impossible to confirm this black and white judgement, and Alfred Fabre-Luce's judgement in *L'Histoire démaquillée,*

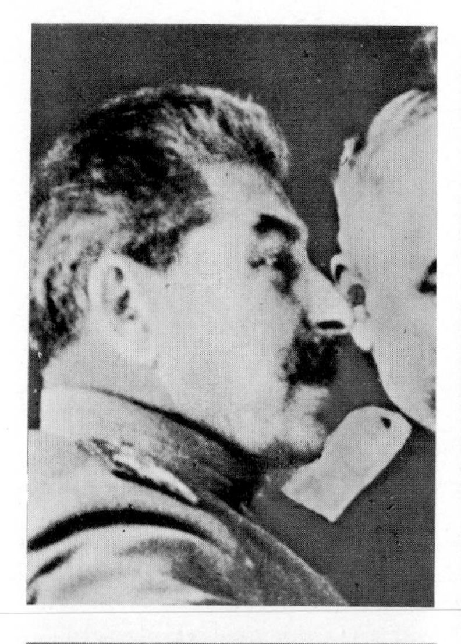

▵ *Stalin and Roosevelt. The latter, now a very sick man, unwittingly allowed himself to be used as Stalin's pawn in destroying the strength of the Western alliance.*

"Churchill changed tack too late", seems more correct. All the same, he changed tack a year before Truman.

The resolutions

We may now quote the resolutions adopted by Churchill, Roosevelt, and Stalin and drawn up by Eden, Stettinius, and Molotov. We shall limit our comments to the resolutions on Poland, Germany, and the Far East.

(a) The reorganisation of Poland

Stalin conceded to the Allies that the Soviet-Polish frontier could in places run three and even five miles to the east of the Curzon Line, which he claimed had been originated by Clemenceau, although neither the British nor the Americans pointed out this obvious historical error. The Oder and the Neisse were to constitute the western frontier of the new Poland. But although, at Teheran, they had agreed on the eastern Neisse (which runs through the town of Neisse), as is clear from a question from Churchill concerning the allocation of the upper Silesian industrial basin, Stalin and Molotov claimed they had been referring to the western Neisse, which meets the Oder between Guben and Fürstenberg.

Churchill pointed out in vain that this additional modification of the German-Polish frontier would entail the further expulsion of eight million Germans. Stalin replied that the matter was now settled, as the province's inhabitants had fled from the Soviet advance, which was only half true, and they then went on to consider the agenda.

As regards Poland's political reorganisation, we must refer to Point 7 of the protocol recorded on February 11 by the foreign ministers of the Big Three. Taking into consideration the Red Army's complete "liberation" of Poland, it stated:

"The provisional government actually operating in Poland must in the future be reorganised on a larger democratic base, to include the popular leaders actually in Poland and those abroad. This new government is to be called the Polish Government of National Unity.

"Mr. Molotov, Mr. Harriman, and Sir A. Clark Kerr are authorised to form a commission to consult initially the members of the Provisional Polish Government, as well as other Polish leaders (both in Poland and abroad), with a view to the reorganisation of the actual government along the lines set out below. The Polish Government of National Unity must set about organising free and open elections as soon as possible, on the basis of a univer-

Anthony Eden, the British Foreign Secretary at the time of the Yalta Conference, was born in 1897 and served on the Western Front in World War I. He was Minister for League of Nations Affairs in 1933 and took over from Sir Samuel Hoare as Foreign Secretary in December. He resigned as a result of the weak British attitude to Italy in 1938. Eden became Dominions Secretary, Secretary of State for War, and finally Foreign Secretary in Churchill's Coalition Government in the War. He proved himself a very able diplomat with a flair for persuasion.

△ *The post-war settlement of Poland agreed at Yalta. In effect the country was shifted to the west, losing her eastern areas but gaining new western ones from Germany.*

sal franchise and a secret ballot. All democratic and anti-Nazi parties will have the right to take part and put up candidates."

It can be seen that there is a great difference between this tripartite declaration and Stalin's statement to Roosevelt on May 4, 1943: "As regards the Hitlerites' rumours on the possibility that a new Polish government will be formed in the U.S.S.R., it is scarcely necessary to give the lie to these ravings."

The two Western powers did not expressly recognise the government formed from the Lublin Committee, but they took note of its existence, and the men who were to give it the character of national unity provided for by the protocol gathered round it and not round the legal government in London. No one stated how many of these men were to come from London and how many from Lublin; but this question was to be examined by a commission and Molotov, who was to be at its centre, would have much greater authority than the British and American Ambassadors in Moscow.

(b) Germany's fate

In order to snatch these concessions from his allies, in exchange for a more vague promise of "free and open elections on the basis of a universal franchise and a secret ballot", Stalin put forward the argument that in the event of a German revival the Soviet Union's security demanded the existence of an independent and friendly Poland. In this respect, it is odd to note that neither Churchill nor Roosevelt thought of pointing out to Stalin that the arrangements they had just decided on for the treatment of Germany eliminated any danger of aggression on her part for centuries to come.

Apart from the Oder-Neisse frontier which was to be imposed on Germany, Point 3 of the Yalta protocol is absolutely clear in this respect. Churchill and Eden with some difficulty secured France's

▵ *Warsaw after the Rising: in the course of the fighting the city was almost completely destroyed, and afterwards the Germans moved in forced labour and tidied the ruins into great piles of bricks.*

right to take part in the occupation of Germany and to send delegates to sit on the Allied Control Commission charged with administering the defeated power. In spite of the treaty he had just signed with General de Gaulle, Stalin at first refused this in terms that were most offensive to France.

As for Roosevelt, he wavered between these two opposing points of view and finally sided with Churchill; but it was agreed that the French occupation zone would be cut out of the British and American zones. It was at this point in the discussions that Roosevelt, in reply to one of Stalin's questions, made a blunder by telling him that he could not possibly obtain authorisation from Congress to maintain American troops in Europe for more than two years after the end of the war. Stalin, it can readily be imagined, found this statement most helpful to his cause.

It was agreed between Roosevelt and Stalin that Germany should pay 20,000 million dollars in reparations; half of this sum would go to the Soviet Union, which would be paid in kind in the form of a transfer of industrial equipment, annual goods deliveries, and the use of German manpower. The final settlement of reparations owed by Germany, and their distribution among the nations that suffered as a result of her aggression, would be determined by a commission in Moscow. Great Britain had reserved her position on the question of the figure of 20,000 million dollars agreed by the Soviets and the Americans.

The principle of dividing Germany up was recorded in the protocol of February 11, and was not clarified during the Yalta discussions; the commission set up under Eden's chairmanship to examine the problem received no directives from the Big Three. It has been assumed from this silence that it was Stalin's intention to transform the Soviet occupation zone into a Communist state which would be Moscow's satellite. Undoubtedly there is much evidence for this assumption.

(c) The Far East

As Russia's relations with Japan were governed by the non-aggression pact signed in Moscow on April 13, 1941, the question of Russia taking part in the war being waged by the Anglo-Americans against the Japanese was settled by a special protocol which was kept secret.

As a reward for its intervention, the U.S.S.R. was to recover the rights it had lost by the Treaty of Portsmouth (U.S.A.) in 1905 which had crowned the Emperor Meiji's victory over Tsar Nicholas

II. As a consequence, it was to regain possession of the southern part of Sakhalin island, the Manchuria railway, the port of Dairen (Lü-ta) which was to be internationalised, and its lease of Port Arthur. In addition, the Russians would receive the Kurile islands, which they had surrendered to Japan in 1875 in exchange for the southern part of Sakhalin island.

It is clear that the agreement of February 11, 1945 took little account of the interests of the fourth great power, Chiang Kai-shek's China. Admittedly it was agreed that the eastern China and southern Manchuria railways would be run jointly by a Soviet-Chinese company and that China would retain "full and complete sovereignty" in Manchuria. Nevertheless the power mainly involved in this arrangement had taken no part in the negotiations, and had not even been consulted. On this matter, the agreement merely stated:

"It is agreed that the arrangements for Outer Mongolia, as well as for the ports and railways mentioned will require the assent of Generalissimo Chiang Kai-shek. The President will take the necessary measures to obtain this assent, acting on the advice of Marshal Stalin."

But the agreement did not state what would happen if the Chunking government refused its agreement. Moreover, the British and American negotiations about this arrangement lost sight of the fact that as in 1898, the Russian reoccupation of Port Arthur and Dairen in the Kuantung peninsula automatically raised the question of Korea. However, Korea does not appear in the text.

President Roosevelt relied on his own intuition, and did not heed the warnings of Ambassador William Bullitt: "Bill, I am not challenging your facts; they are correct. I am not challenging the logic of your argument. But I have the feeling that Stalin isn't that kind of man. Harry [Hopkins] says he isn't and that all he wants is his country's security. And I think that if I give him all I can give him, and ask for nothing in return, *noblesse oblige,* he won't try to annex anything and he will agree to work with me for a world of democracy and peace."

△ *But in Germany too the rubble was piling up, the result of ever more efficient Allied bombing.*
Overleaf: *The harrowing sight that greeted the Allies as they advanced into Germany–the pitiable survivors of the concentration camps.*

CHAPTER 145
Himmler's offensive

▲ *General Leclerc (wearing the* képi*) inspects the men and the machines of his French 2nd Armoured Division. After helping in the defence of Strasbourg during Operation* "Nordwind", *the division was moved south as part of the French II Corps for the crushing of the Colmar pocket.*

Before he could accept the German surrender, the offer of which was to be brought to him at Rheims by a delegation headed by Colonel-General Jodl, General Eisenhower still had to repel two attacks, one directed against his own authority, and the other against the 6th Army Group in lower Alsace.

On December 28, 1944, Eisenhower went to Hasselt, where Montgomery had set up his headquarters. He wanted to go over the plans for future operations with him, to begin as soon as the Ardennes pocket had been nipped off. Eisenhower and Montgomery had no difficulty in reaching agreement on the objective to be set for the offensive they were about to launch. Both favoured the Ruhr. But Montgomery thought that the "major crisis" that had just been resolved authorised him to adopt the claim he had pressed at the beginning of the preceding August. He wanted control of operations, and he thought himself the more qualified to bear the responsibility since Eisenhower had put the American 1st and 9th Armies under his command. Hence his letter to "Ike", dated December 29. Point 6 of this read:

"I suggest that your directive should finish with this sentence:

"'12 and 21 Army Groups will develop operations in accordance with the above instructions.

"'From now onwards full operational direction, control, and co-ordination of these operations is vested in the C.-in-C. 21 Army Group, subject to such instructions as may be issued by the Supreme Commander from time to time.'"

In writing this, Montgomery was disregarding the prudent advice contained in Brooke's letter of December 24 to him:

"I would like to give you a word of warning. Events and enemy action have forced on Eisenhower the setting up of a more satisfactory system of command. I feel it is most important that you should not even in the slightest degree appear to rub this undoubted fact in to anyone at S.H.A.E.F. or elsewhere."

Eisenhower rejected his subordinate's suggestion by return of post. But, even had he not done this on his own initiative, he would have been ordered to do so by General Marshall, who cabled him from Washington on December 30:

"They may or may not have brought to your attention articles in certain London papers proposing a British deputy commander for all your ground forces and implying that you have undertaken too much of a task yourself. My feeling is this: under no circumstances make any concessions of any kind whatsoever. I am not assuming that you had in mind such a concession I just wish you to be certain of our attitude. You are doing a grand job, and go on and give them hell."

The matter would have stopped there if, on January 5, 1945, Montgomery had not given a press conference on the Battle of the Ardennes, which drove the American generals to the limit of exasperation. The text of the conference was published by General Bradley and it can be said that although Montgomery polished his own image and took some pleasure in exaggerating the part played by British forces in the Ardennes, he did not criticise his allies or their leaders in any way. But the journalists accredited to S.H.A.E.F. and army group seized on his speech and commented bitterly on it, some standing up for Montgomery, others for Eisenhower.

The crisis reached flashpoint when Bradley informed his old friend Eisenhower that he would ask to be recalled to the United States rather than serve under Montgomery's command. In view of the rumours spread by Goebbels's propaganda services, Churchill thought he ought to step in, which he did in the House of Commons on January 18. His excellent speech made special mention of the all-important part that the U.S. Army had played in the battle and placated everyone.

Besides this, another move of the Prime Minister's contributed to relieving the tension between S.H.A.E.F. and the 21st Army Group. As operations in Italy had slowed down considerably, it was suggested that Alexander was being wasted there. So Eisenhower's deputy, Tedder, was to be recalled to ordinary R.A.F. service, his place being taken by Alexander. Though this compromise did not win Eisenhower's approval, it also came up against Montgomery's decided opposition. If he could not control operations himself, he did not want to see anybody else get the job. From this point of view, he thought that nothing should be changed in the pattern of command.

Himmler's offensive

During the night of December 31/January

▷ *Armoured vehicles (in the foreground Stuart light tanks) of the French Foreign Legion parade through the streets of Strasbourg.*

△▷ *Strasbourg Cathedral on the day of the city's liberation.*

1, Himmler, as commander of Army Group *"Oberrhein"*, unleashed Operation *"Nordwind"*, giving his troops as objective the Saverne gap. In this way the American 7th Army would be cut in two and its fighting troops in the Bitche–Lauterbourg–Strasbourg salient annihilated. After the fast advance that Patton had been ordered to make on December 19, General Patch had had to extend his left flank as far as Saint Avold and, in the threatened sector, could only field VI Corps against eight German divisions, including the 21st Panzer and the 17th *"Götz von Berlichingen"* S.S. *Panzergrenadier* Divisions.

When he had redeployed as ordered (which stretched the seven divisions of the 7th Army over a front of 90 miles), the commander of the 6th Army Group, General Devers, had naturally been concerned about what to do in the event of a German offensive. In agreement with S.H.A.E.F., he had provided in such an event for his forces to fall back on the eastern slopes of the Vosges and the Belfort gap. This implied abandoning the plain of Alsace. In the afternoon of January 1, after a telephone call from Eisenhower, he issued the order to begin the movements planned for this eventuality.

de Gaulle disapproves

As Chief-of-Staff to the French Ministry of National Defence, General Juin had been advised since December 28 of the intentions of the 6th Army Group, confirmed by S.H.A.E.F. He had immediately informed General de Gaulle. The latter, seeing the possibility approach, wrote to General Eisenhower on January 1:

"For its part, the French Government cannot allow Strasbourg to fall into enemy hands again without doing everything in its power to defend it."

At the same time, he gave General de Lattre the following order:

"In the event of Allied forces falling

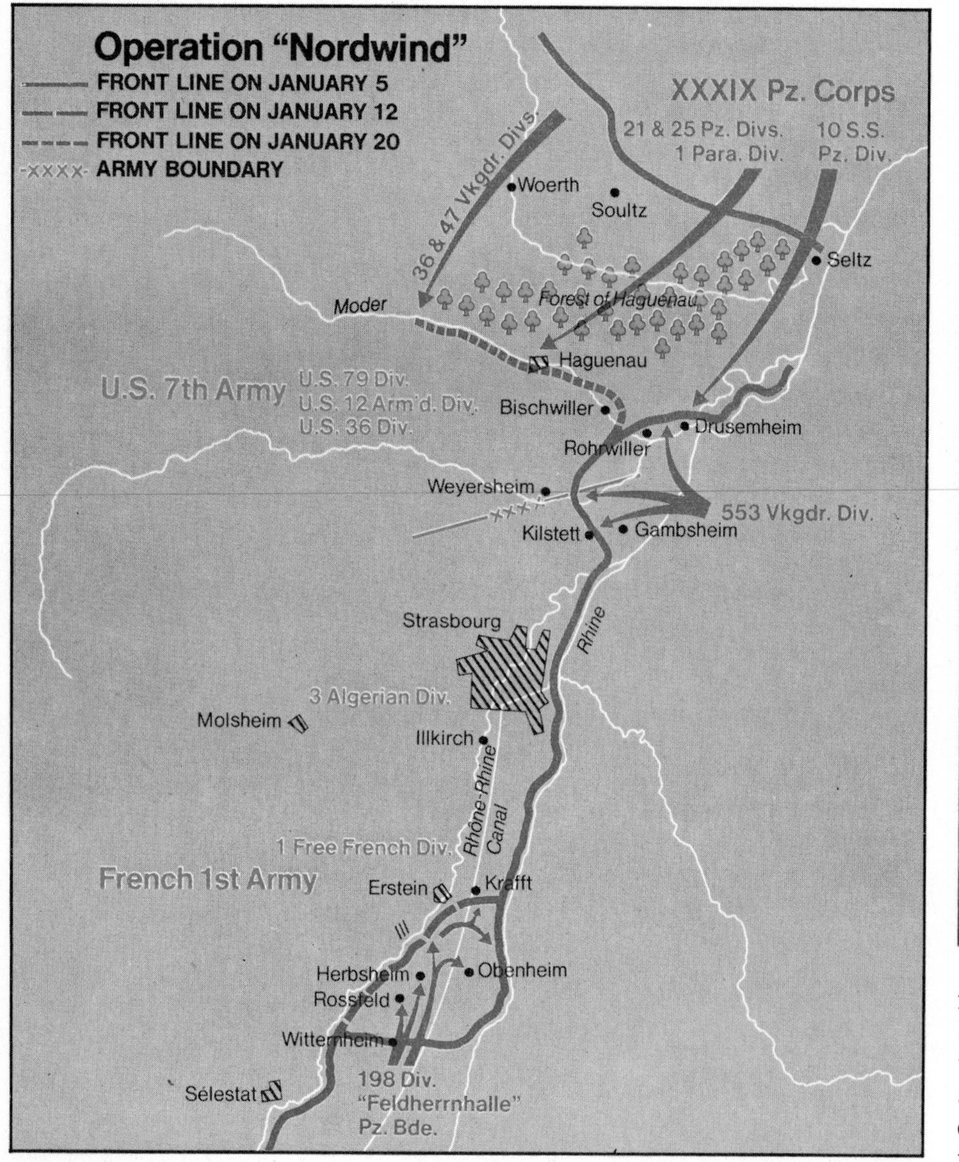

Première Armée Française

A LA POPULATION DE STRASBOURG

La Première Armée Française à désormais la mission de défendre votre Cité, chère entre toutes à nos âmes de soldats.

Le Général de GAULLE, Président du Gouvernement Provisoire de la République, Chef des Armées Françaises, voulu que ce soit notre Armée qui protège STRASBOURG.

Je fais ici la solennelle promesse qu'elle se montrera digne de cette tâche : elle veillera sur vous, fidèlement et avec fierté.

J'adresse à votre vaillante population, à laquelle j'ai donné depuis longtemps tout mon cœur, un salut affectueux et un message de confiance.

Le Général de Division DU VIGIER a été nommé Gouverneur Militaire et Commandant de la 10e Région. C'est le Chef valeureux qui, avec la 1re Division blindée, est parvenu le premier au Rhin. Dès aujourd'hui, il prend la charge qu'assumait provisoirement le Général SCHWARTZ. Celui-ci, dont vous avez pu apprécier toutes les qualités, reste parmi vous, comme Commandant de la Subdivision du Bas-Rhin.

Ainsi STRASBOURG, délivrée hier par les soldats français de la 2e Division Blindée du Général LECLERC, est à nouveau défendue, depuis le 6 janvier, par l'Armée Française.

Confiance, Strasbourgeois ! Répondant avec enthousiasme à l'appel de notre Chef, le Général DE GAULLE, nous saurons forcer la victoire !

P. C., le 6 Janvier 1945.

Le Général d'Armée DE LATTRE DE TASSIGNY

Commandant en Chef la Première Armée française

J. DE LATTRE

△ *Operation* "Nordwind", Reichsführer-*S.S. Heinrich Himmler's ill-advised offensive against Strasbourg.*

△▷ *General de Lattre de Tassigny's proclamation to the citizens of Strasbourg on January 6, 1945. It called for calm and confidence, and pledged the French 1st Army to the successful defence of the city.*

back from their present positions to the north of the French 1st Army, I instruct you to act on your own and take over the defence of Strasbourg."

These letters had gone when General de Gaulle was advised of the order to withdraw that had been circulated by General Devers. On receiving the news, he cabled President Roosevelt and the Prime Minister to make clear that he was opposed to evacuating Strasbourg and he instructed General Juin to express the same opinion at S.H.A.E.F.

The interview between Juin and General Bedell Smith, who met him the next day at S.H.A.E.F., was stormy, as was to be expected from two such plain-spoken men. There were even threats about what would happen if the French 1st Army removed itself from the authority of General Devers. All the same, noted Juin:

"Bedell Smith, who had blanched, nevertheless seemed to want to help and assured me before I left that he would try once more to convince his superior and I secured an interview for General de Gaulle with General Eisenhower the next day."

On receiving the report prepared for him by Juin, de Gaulle once more appealed against the S.H.A.E.F. decision which, he had just learned, affected not only Strasbourg but the entire plain of Alsace. In particular, he wrote to Eisenhower on January 3:

"In any case, I must confirm that the French Government cannot accept that Alsace and a part of Lorraine should be intentionally evacuated without fighting, so to speak, especially since the French Army occupies most of the area. To agree to such an evacuation and in such conditions would be an error from the point of view of the general conduct of the war, which stems not only from the military command, but also from the Allied governments. It would also be a serious error from the French national point of view, to which the government is answerable.

"Therefore I have once more to instruct General de Lattre to use the French forces he has to defend the positions he now occupies and also to defend Strasbourg, even if the American forces on his left withdraw.

"From my point of view, I am extremely sorry that this disagreement has occurred at a serious moment and I should like to hope that we can resolve our differences."

In *Crusade in Europe*, General Eisenhower mentions this incident and writes that:

"At first glance de Gaulle's argument seemed to be based upon political considerations founded more on emotion than on logic and consideration."

This represents the typical reasoning of the American strategist of the time, according to whom a military leader should not consider any objective but the destruction of the enemy's organised forces, without regard for political, geographical, sentimental, or prestige aims. In short, his thought regarding Strasbourg was the same as it had been before Paris the previous summer, and as it would be before Berlin three months later. Nevertheless, against this same point of view, he had to think of the consequences that a Franco-American crisis could have on Allied relations.

▲ G.I.s catch up with their mail and with the news while waiting for the German offensive to break on them. Although he at first advocated the abandonment of the plain of Alsace, Eisenhower was at last persuaded by General de Gaulle's political objections to change his mind and order the American 7th Army to hold the Moder line.

Churchill sides with de Gaulle

Churchill had been alerted by de Gaulle and, accompanied by Brooke, travelled to Paris. According to Brooke, they found Eisenhower "most depressed looking" when they walked down the steps from the plane, and it is certain that, at the lunch that followed, the Prime Minister was preaching to one already half-converted. A few hours later, Generals de Gaulle and Juin met Eisenhower, in the presence of Bedell Smith, Churchill, and Brooke, who noted that very evening:

"De Gaulle painted a gloomy picture of the massacres that would ensue if the Germans returned to portions of Alsace-Lorraine. However, Ike had already decided to alter his dispositions so as to leave the divisions practically where they were and not to withdraw the two divisions that were to have been moved up into Patton's reserve."

Juin confirms this: "When General de Gaulle and I arrived at Eisenhower's headquarters at Versailles . . . Churchill was already there. As soon as we came in he informed us that it was all settled and that Strasbourg would not be abandoned. There was not even any discussion, and the only thing that was decided was that I should go with General Bedell Smith the next day to Vittel to inform General Devers, commanding the 6th Army Group."

Moreover, the tension between Eisenhower and de Gaulle eased so much as soon as this incident was settled that Eisenhower could not restrain himself from confiding to de Gaulle the difficulties he was having with Montgomery.

The battle for Strasbourg

Both on his own initiative and in virtue of the orders he received from Paris, General de Lattre was absolutely determined to hold Strasbourg. And so, on the night of January 2-3, he promptly sent in the solid 3rd Algerian Division, under the command of General du Vigier, recently appointed governor of the city. But, in spite of this, de Lattre intended to remain as long as he could under the control of General Devers and not make difficulties

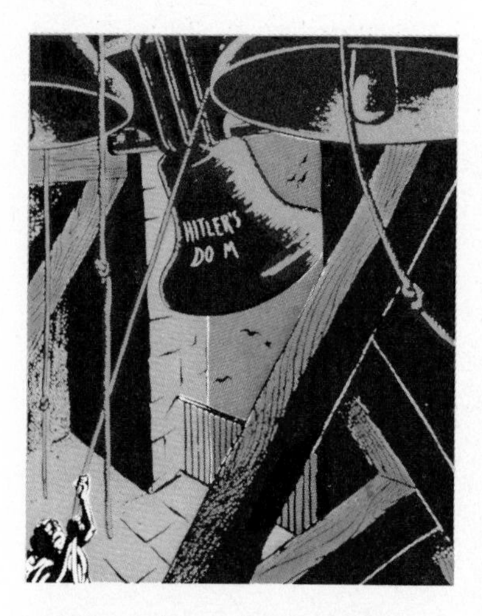

▵ *"For whom tolls the bell?" "It tolls death for Hitler." And with the Allies on the Rhine and Oder, the defeat of the Third Reich and Hitler's suicide were only weeks away.*

for inter-Allied strategy. That is why, at 2200 hours on January 3, he was very happy to receive the signal announcing that the 6th Army Group had received new orders.

As a result, the American VI Corps, between the Rhine and the Sarre, received orders to continue its retreat only as far as the Moder. But, on January 5, while VI Corps was digging in at this position and the 3rd Algerian Division completed its positions in Strasbourg, the 553rd *Volksgrenadier* Division crossed the Rhine at Gambsheim, between Strasbourg and the confluence of the Moder and Rhine. The next day, it was the turn of the German 19th Army to go over to the offensive, from the Colmar bridgehead. Pressing between the Ill and the Rhône-Rhine Canal, the *"Feldherrnhalle"* Panzer Brigade and the 198th Division managed to get as far as the Erstein heights, less than 13 miles from Strasbourg and 20 from the Gambsheim bridgehead that the 553rd Division had extended as far as the village of Killstett.

Around Strasbourg, attack and counter-attack followed ceaselessly. The Germans had forced the Moder a little above Haguenau and for a short time managed to establish a link with their 553rd Division. However, on January 26, they had definitely lost it again and the battlefield fell silent. O.B. West was very unhappy with the tactics Himmler had used in this offensive, for, instead of wearing down the enemy, he had wasted 11 divisions, four of them of the *Waffen*-S.S., frittering them away in piecemeal actions, ignoring the fact that the barrier of the Rhine prevented him from co-ordinating their movements. All the same, it was General Wiese who paid for the failure of *"Nordwind"*. He received the order to hand over command of the 19th Army to his comrade Rasp. As for Himmler, his flattering promotion to the command of Army Group "Vistula" led, on January 28, to the appointment of Colonel-General Hausser, still recuperating from the wounds he had received during the bloody fighting in the Falaise pocket, to command of Army Group *"Oberrhein"*.

In spite of Operation *"Nordwind"*, on January 15 de Lattre signed his "Personal and Secret Instruction Number 7":

"Leave the Germans no chance of escape. Free Colmar undamaged. The task consists of strangling the pocket alongside the Rhine where it receives its supplies, that is around Brisach.

"Two convergent wedges will be driven in this direction. The first will go northward and will be made by Béthouart's I Corps, which will throw the enemy off balance and suck in his reserves. Then, two days later, II Corps will go into action. This staggering is required by the time it will take to get the expected reserves into place. Its effect will be to increase the surprise of the enemy. Between the two offensive blocs, in the high Vosges, the front will remain inactive at the beginning. It will begin to move when our net along the Rhine is so tightly stretched that the fish is ready to be pulled in."

At this time, Devers and Eisenhower were so concerned about cutting off the Colmar pocket quickly that they did not hesitate to provide substantial reinforcements for the French 1st Army: the U.S. 3rd Division remained under its command, and it also received, though with certain limitations, the 28th Division and the 12th Armoured Division (Major-Generals Norman D. Cota and Roderik R. Allen), as well as the French 2nd Armoured Division under Leclerc, transferred from the Strasbourg area specifically for this purpose.

So, by January 20, 1945, the forces available to de Lattre amounted to 12 divisions, four of which were armoured. However, it should be pointed out that the 3rd Algerian Division was still engaged in and around Killstett and did not take part in the battle of Colmar and that, in the high Vosges, the newly-created 10th Division (General Billotte) was restricted to the modest rôle described above.

The German defence

Facing these forces along the 100-mile long Alsace bridgehead, the German 19th Army deployed its LXIV and LXIII Corps north and south under the command, respectively, of General Thumm and Lieutenant-General Abraham. The two corps had seven infantry or mountain divisions and the 106th *"Feldherrnhalle"* Panzer Brigade. But these forces were threadbare. Including the reinforcements attached to them, the best-equipped (the 198th Division: Colonel Barde) had exactly 6,891 men in the line, and the 716th *Volksgrenadier* Division (Colonel Hafner) had only 4,546. Furthermore, although de Lattre complained about not receiving all the supplies he thought

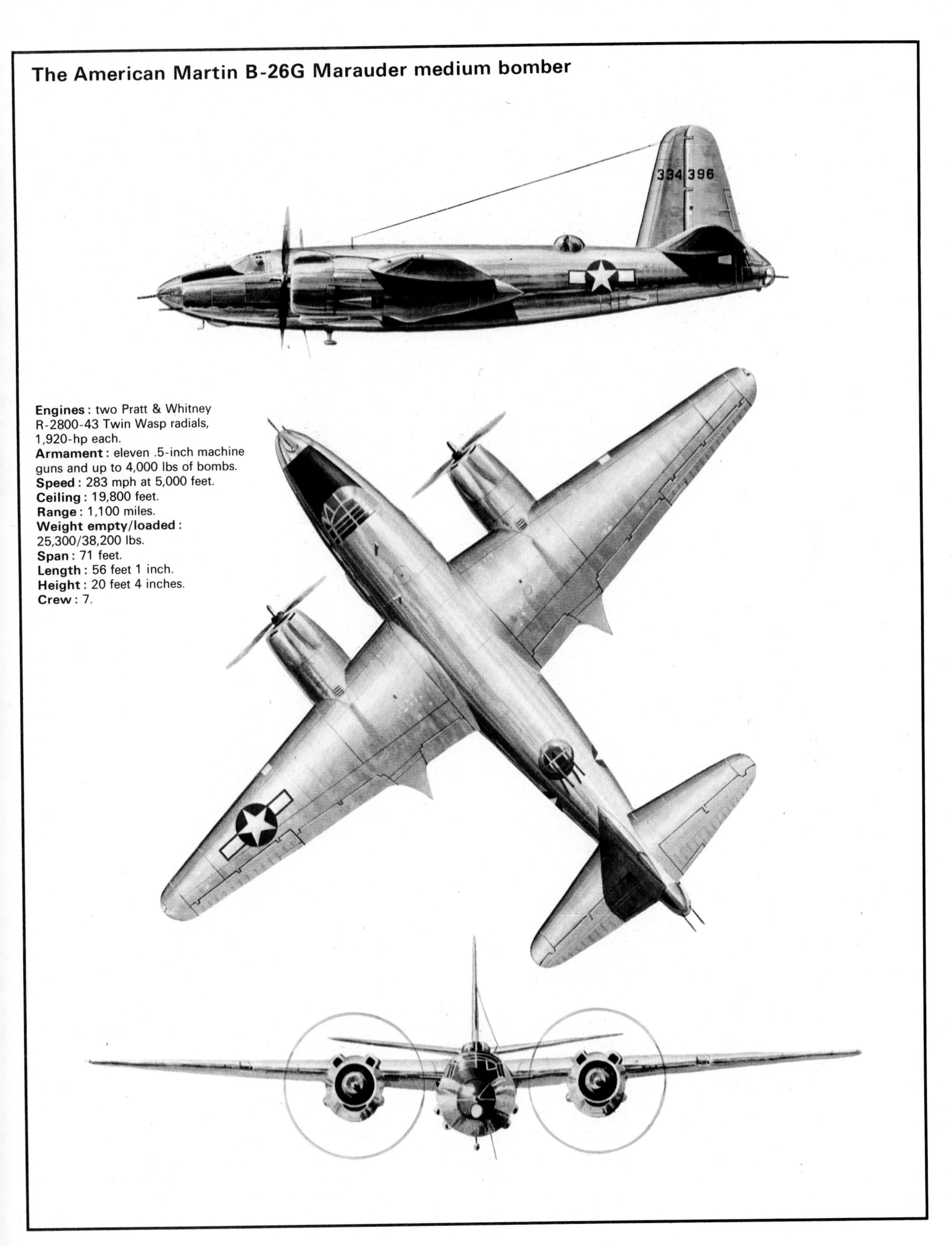
The American Martin B-26G Marauder medium bomber
334396
Engines: two Pratt & Whitney R-2800-43 Twin Wasp radials, 1,920-hp each.
Armament: eleven .5-inch machine guns and up to 4,000 lbs of bombs.
Speed: 283 mph at 5,000 feet.
Ceiling: 19,800 feet.
Range: 1,100 miles.
Weight empty/loaded: 25,300/38,200 lbs.
Span: 71 feet.
Length: 56 feet 1 inch.
Height: 20 feet 4 inches.
Crew: 7.

▷ *An M3 half-track of the French 1st Army moves into Colmar on February 2, 1945.*
▷▷ *A mine explodes in the path of an M10 tank destroyer of a French armoured division, fully equipped with the latest U.S.* matériel.

he needed, by the eighth day of battle General Rasp was reduced to ordering strict economy to his gunners: 12 15-cm and 15 10.5-cm shells per day per gun, compared with 90 155-mm and 120 105-mm shells in the French 1st Army.

Three circumstances, however, compensated a little for the numerical and *matériel* inferiority of the defenders:

1. the terrain, which was no more than "a network of streams and rivers" according to de Lattre. Within it are many woods and even more villages, among which should be mentioned the manufacturing and industrial towns of the Mulhouse region;
2. the weather. On the first day, I Corps attacked LXIII Corps in the face of a snowstorm blowing from the north-east. At night, the temperature fell to 20 and even 25 degrees Centigrade below zero. Finally, just when German resistance was softening, an unexpected rise in the temperature swelled the rivers and made the roads into sloughs of mud; and
3. though far less numerous, the Panther tanks and *"Jagdpanther"* and *"Nashorn"* tank destroyers, with their very high velocity 8.8-cm guns, were far superior to the French 1st Army's Sherman tanks and M10 tank destroyers. This superiority was emphasised by the German vehicles' wide tracks, which allowed them to manoeuvre on the snow in weather conditions with which their opponents were not able to cope.

At 0700 hours on January 20, H-hour sounded for the reinforced I Corps. Its task was to break the enemy line between Thann and the Forest of Nünenbruck, to capture Cernay, and then to push on without stopping towards Ensisheim and Réguisheim on the Ill. For this purpose, over a 14-mile front, Béthouart had the 9th Colonial Division (General Morlière) around Mulhouse, the 2nd Moroccan Division (General Carpentier) in the centre, and the 4th Moroccan Mountain Division (General de Hesdin) around Thann. In spite of the support of the tanks of the 1st Armoured Division (General Sudre), the attempt to break the enemy lines towards Cernay was not very successful, both because of the tough resistance met, aided by well-sited minefields, and because of the snowstorms which made artillery observation impossible.

On the other hand, the secondary attack, which had been entrusted to the 9th Colonial Division, took the villages of Burtzwiller, Illzach, Kingersheim, Pfastadt, and Lutterbach, a remarkable success due to the dash with which General Salan had led the infantry of this division.

On the following day, LXIII Corps counter-attacked and, on January 22, with the storm blowing worse than ever, General Béthouart expressed the opinion that they should wait for it to blow itself out. But any let-up on the part of I Corps would have prejudiced the attack of II

△ *"Our armies are marching with all despatch to the East and to the West . . ." "Is that really true?" "Yes,* mein Führer, *the ones on the Western Front to the East, and the ones on the Eastern Front to the West!"*

Corps, which was just finishing its preparations. So Béthouart was ordered to press on with his attack, and a fierce, bitter struggle was waged close to Wittelsheim, in the Forest of Nünenbruck, and for the factory towns with their potassium deposits. These towns had to be cleared one by one.

The Colmar pocket wiped out

On January 23, II Corps, still under the command of General G. de Monsabert, forced a second wedge into the German line. This was achieved with more ease than the first, even though General Rasp had got wind of the French plans.

On the right, the American 3rd Division had taken Ostheim. On the left, the 1st Free French Division had fought bitterly to capture the village of Illhausern and had formed a bridgehead on the right bank of the Ill, thus preparing to outflank Colmar to the north. But LXIV Corps stiffened its resistance and counterattacked, preventing Monsabert from any swift exploitation of his success towards Neuf-Brisach. LXIII Corps was likewise preventing Béthouart from moving on. Hidden in the woods, or even inside houses, the Panzers exacted a heavy toll from the men of the 2nd and 5th Armoured Divisions, supporting the infantry. However, on January 27, the U.S. 3rd Division reached the Colmar Canal, while General Garbay's 1st Free French Division, reinforced by Colonel Faure's paratroops, took the villages of Jebsheim and Grussenheim. Seeing how serious the situation had become, O.K.W. authorised Rasp to pull the 198th Division back over the Rhine, i.e. to give up all the ground won between Rhinau and Erstein by the attack of January 7.

Wishing to press on and complete the attack, General Devers, at the request of the commander of the French 1st Army, put XXI Corps (Major-General Frank W. Milburn) under his command, as well as the U.S. 75th Division (Major-General Porter). Milburn, who from this time on commanded all the American forces involved in the offensive, and the French 5th Armoured Division, was ordered to position his forces between Monsabert's II Corps and Billotte's 10th Division, and then push on towards Neuf-

△ *General Emile Béthouart, commander of the French I Corps. Operating on the south side of the Colmar pocket, his troops initially had a very hard time of it, and Béthouart wished to call off his attack. But de Lattre ordered him to press on regardless so that German forces would not be able to switch to the northern sector, where General de Monsabert's II Corps was about to launch its offensive.*

Brisach and also south towards Ensisheim to meet Béthouart. The offensive began again. In the evening of January 30, after a terrifying artillery bombardment of 16,438 105-mm and 155-mm shells, the United States 3rd Division (Major-General O'Daniel) succeeded in crossing the Colmar Canal, and this allowed the United States 28th Division to advance as far as the suburbs of Colmar. The division did not enter Colmar itself, for at the gates of the city, which had been left intact, General Norman D. Cota was courteous enough to give that honour to his comrade-in-arms Schlesser, commanding the 4th Combat Command (5th Armoured Division).

The United States 12th Armoured Division sped south to exploit its victory, with the intention of linking up with I Corps, which had taken Ensisheim, Soultz, and Guebwiller on February 4 and then pushed its 1st Armoured Division and 4th Moroccan Mountain Division forward.

The next day, French and American forces linked up at Rouffach and Sainte Croix-en-Plaine. Twenty-four hours later, in the light of searchlights shining towards the night sky, General O'Daniel's infantry "scaled" the ramparts of Neuf-Brisach in the best mediaeval style. Lastly, at 0800 hours on February 9, a deafening explosion told the men of the French 1st and 2nd Armoured Divisions, who were mopping-up the Forest of la Hardt, together with the 2nd Moroccan Division, that the Germans had just blown the Chalampé bridge, on the Mulhouse–Freiburg road, behind them as they pulled back over the Rhine.

And so, at dawn on the 20th day, the battle of Colmar reached its end. General Rasp left 22,010 prisoners, 80 guns, and 70 tanks in the hands of the enemy, but he had succeeded in bringing back over the Rhine some 50,000 men, 7,000 motor vehicles, 1,500 guns, and 60 armoured vehicles, which underlines his personal qualities of leadership.

As for Allied losses, the figures provided by General de Lattre will allow the reader to appreciate the cost of a modern battle. Of a total of 420,000 Allied troops involved (295,000 French, 125,000 American), casualties were as follows:

	French	*American*
Killed	1,595	542
Wounded	8,583	2,670
Sick	3,887	3,228
Totals	14,065	6,440

Considering just the French, de Lattre's figures also show that the infantry had taken the lion's share. On January 20, it had put 60,000 men into the line, that is about a fifth of the men in the 1st Army. On February 9, it could own to three-quarters of the losses, with 1,138 killed and 6,513 wounded. Add to these figures the 354 killed and 1,151 wounded which the battle cost the armoured units, and it becomes clear that the other arms lost only 1,022 killed and wounded. Finally, due credit must be given to the magnificent effort of the medical services under Surgeon-General Guirriec. In spite of the appalling weather they had only 142 deaths, that is 0.9 per cent of the cases received.

As a conclusion to the story of this battle, some tribute should be paid to the men who fought in it. In the *Revue militaire suisse,* Major-General Montfort has written:

"The French, under superb leadership and enjoying powerful *matériel* advantages, made a magnificent effort, fully worthy of their predecessors in World War I.

"The Germans, under extraordinarily difficult conditions and three differing requirements (operational, *matériel,* and morale), defended themselves with great ability and fought . . . with courage worthy of praise."

Montgomery and Eisenhower clash again

It should be noted that there had been much inter-Allied squabbling about the length of time that the battle for Colmar was taking: the Allied high command wanted this irritating pocket cleared out of the way as quickly as possible, so that all available Allied forces might be readied for the last devastating blow against Germany that would win the war in the West. The irritation caused by the Colmar delay was perhaps exacerbated by another clash between Eisenhower and Montgomery. But what increased the trouble even more was the fact that Brooke backed Montgomery with all the weight of his authority. Once more S.H.A.E.F. and the 21st Army Group were divided on the alternatives of the "concentrated push" or the "wide front".

Eisenhower rejected Montgomery's in-

▵ *Shermans of the French 1st Army push on towards the Rhine after the liberation of Colmar.*

tention of supervising Bradley's operations, but nevertheless, on December 31, 1944, informed Montgomery of his plan of operations:

"Basic plan–to destroy enemy forces west of Rhine, north of the Moselle, and to prepare for crossing the Rhine in force with the *main effort north of the Ruhr.*"

Once the Ardennes salient had been pinched out (Point *a*), Eisenhower envisaged the following general offensive:

"*b.* Thereafter First and Third Armies to drive to north-east on general line Prum-Bonn, eventually to Rhine.

"*c.* When *a* is accomplished, 21st Army Group, with Ninth U.S. Army under operational command, to resume preparations for 'Veritable'."

In practical terms, this plan required Montgomery to force the Reichswald forest position, which bars the corridor between the Maas and the Rhine on the Dutch-German frontier, to secure the left bank of the Rhine between Emmerich and Düsseldorf, and to prepare to force a passage of the river north of its junction with the Ruhr. This sketch of a plan pleased Montgomery, who wrote:

"It did all I wanted except in the realm of operational control, and because of Marshall's telegram that subject was closed. It put the weight in the north and gave the Ninth American Army to 21 Army Group. It gave me power of decision in the event of disagreement with Bradley on the boundary between 12 and 21 Army Groups. In fact, I had been given very nearly all that I had been asking for since August. Better late than never. I obviously could not ask for more."

Nevertheless, when one considers the allotment of forces and in particular the fixing of objectives, there is no avoiding the fact that the two sides did not speak a common language any more.

Actually, Montgomery estimated that if "Veritable" was to be successful, American reinforcements should consist of five corps, (16 divisions), of which four corps (13 divisions) should be placed under the command of the American 9th Army, and the rest under the British 2nd Army. In these estimates, he seems to have been completely unaware of the principles established by his superior at the beginning of his outline dated December 31: "to destroy enemy forces west of Rhine". According to Eisenhower's clearly-expressed opinion, this required a second push from around Prüm towards the Rhine at Bonn, which would reduce the United States forces which could be detached for "Veritable"

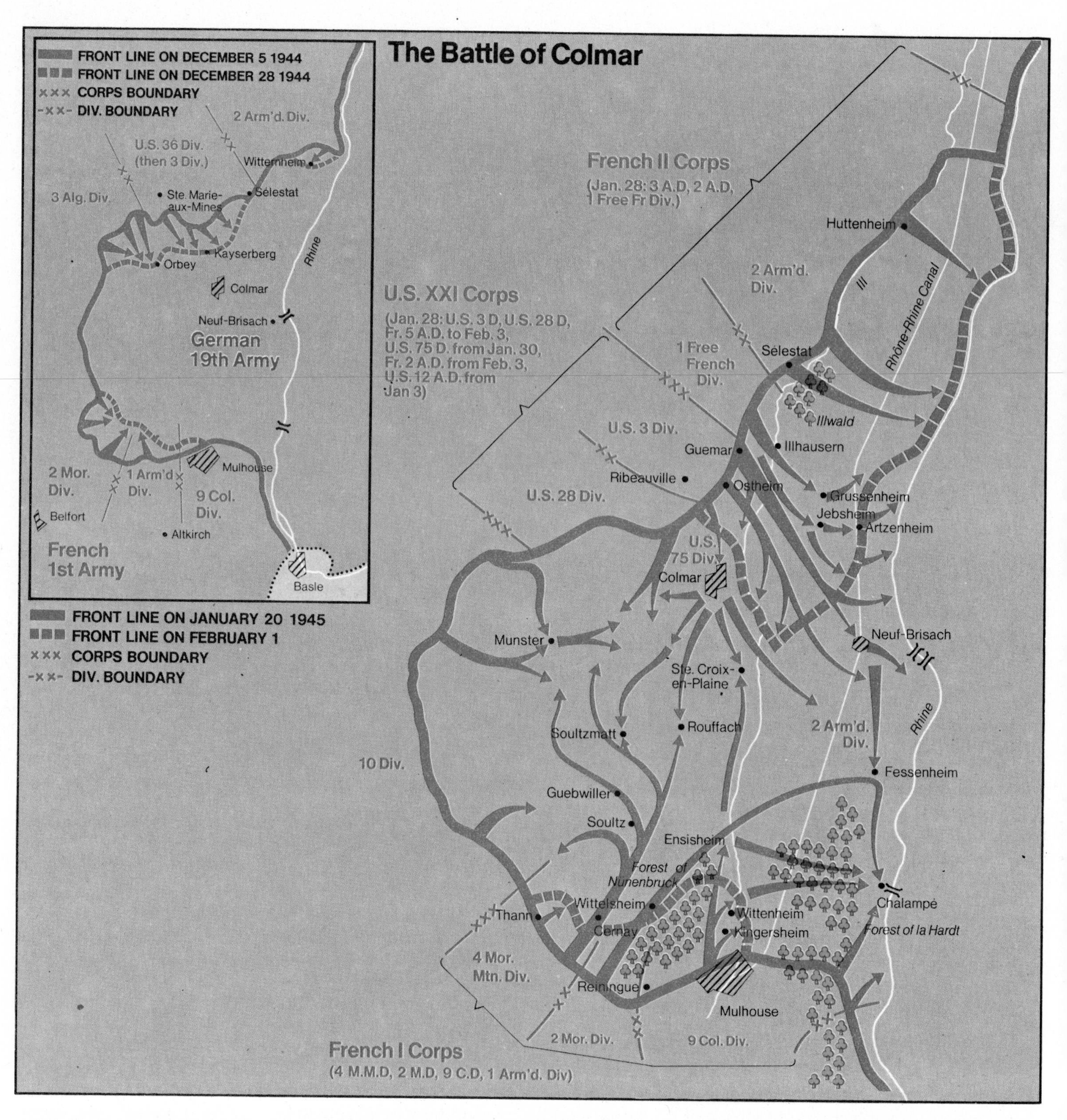

△ *The French 1st Army's battle to eliminate the German 19th Army's pocket around Colmar.*

to only three corps and 12 divisions.

Montgomery was obliged to give in, but he resumed the argument on January 20 when he heard the news that Bradley, far from limiting himself to reducing the Ardennes salient, intended to follow up his attack for another fortnight. Montgomery wrote to Brooke:

"Both Ike and Bradley are emphatic that we should not–not–cross the Rhine in strength anywhere until we are lined up along its entire length from Nijmegen to Switzerland."

Two days later, in a second letter which, like the first, he has not quoted in his memoirs, he harped on the same question:

"My latest information is that S.H.A.E.F. are very worried about situation in South about Colmar and Strasbourg . . ."

As the commander-in-chief seemed ready to reinforce this sector, it followed that "Veritable" would be postponed indefinitely. This led him to conclude bitterly:

"I fear that the old snags of indecision and vacillation and refusal to consider the military problem fairly and squarely are coming to the front again . . . The real trouble is that there is no control and the three Army Groups are each intent on their own affairs. Patton to-day issued a stirring order to Third Army, saying the next step would be Cologne . . . one has to preserve a sense of humour these days, otherwise one would go mad."

Support for Eisenhower

Brooke was appreciative of this argument and "cordially, but very gravely", as General Eisenhower writes, expressed the view to him that putting his plan into effect would have the result of producing an "organised dispersion" of Allied forces. Eisenhower opposed this view, and events proved him right. First of all, the Germans had to be deprived of the advantage of permanent fortifications which allowed them to economise their means and then build up massive forces in the sector where the main attack would be launched:

"If, however, we should first, in a series of concentrated and powerful attacks, destroy the German forces west of the Rhine, the effect would be to give us all along the great front a defensive line of equal strength to the enemy's. We calculated that with the western bank of the Rhine in our possession we could hurl some seventy-five reinforced divisions against the German in great converging attacks. If we allowed the enemy south of the Ruhr to remain in the Siegfried, we would be limited to a single offensive by some thirty-five divisions.

"A second advantage of our plan would be the deflection of the enemy forces later to be met at the crossings of the Rhine obstacle. Moreover, the effect of the converging attack is multiplied when it is accompanied by such air power as we had in Europe in the early months of 1945. Through its use we could prevent the enemy from switching forces back and forth at will against either of the attacking columns and we could likewise employ our entire air power at any moment to further the advance in any area desired."

But although Eisenhower had refuted Brooke's point, he was unable to convert the latter to his way of thinking. That is why he travelled to Marseilles on January 25 to explain to Marshall, who was on his way to Yalta via Malta, his plan of operations and the objections it was coming up against among the British. He had no difficulty in obtaining Marshall's complete agreement, and the latter said to him at the end of the interview:

"I can, of course, uphold your position merely on the principle that these decisions fall within your sphere of responsibility. But your plan is so sound that I think it better for you to send General Smith to Malta so that he may explain these matters in detail. Their logic will be convincing."

This was done and, after some explanations by Bedell Smith and some amendments on the part of the Combined Chiefs-of-Staff Committee, Eisenhower's plan, comprising of a double push towards the Rhine and a double encirclement of the Ruhr, was adopted and Montgomery would spare nothing to make it a success.

∆∆ American infantry move up through a snowstorm, typical of the weather that helped the Germans considerably at the beginning of 1945.
∆ General Marshall, head of the U.S. Army, arrives in Malta en route to Yalta. Marshall sided firmly with Eisenhower in the dispute the latter was having with Montgomery.

△ *Evidence of American artillery superiority: a destroyed German triple 2-cm self-propelled mounting.*

CHAPTER 146
Remagen Bridge

On January 16, the American 3rd and 1st Armies crushed the tip of the Ardennes salient and linked up in the ruins of Houffalize. The following day, as agreed, the 1st Army was returned to the command of Bradley, to his great satisfaction. But he was far less pleased with the task now given him, that of engaging the Germans in the wooded and hilly region of Schleiden and Schmidt, which had cost him so dear the previous autumn, and of capturing the hydro-electric system of the Rur, the Erft, and the Olef. On February 8, V Corps (under Major-General L. T. Gerow), of the 1st Army had reached its objective. That was that. At dawn, on the next day, the Germans blew up the reservoir gates and from mid-day onwards the water was rising at a rate of nearly two and a half feet an hour in front of the 9th Army.

Meanwhile, the left of this army, still under the command of Lieutenant-General William H. Simpson, and the right of the British 2nd Army, under General Miles C. Dempsey, were taking out the salient which the enemy was holding between the Maas and the Rur,

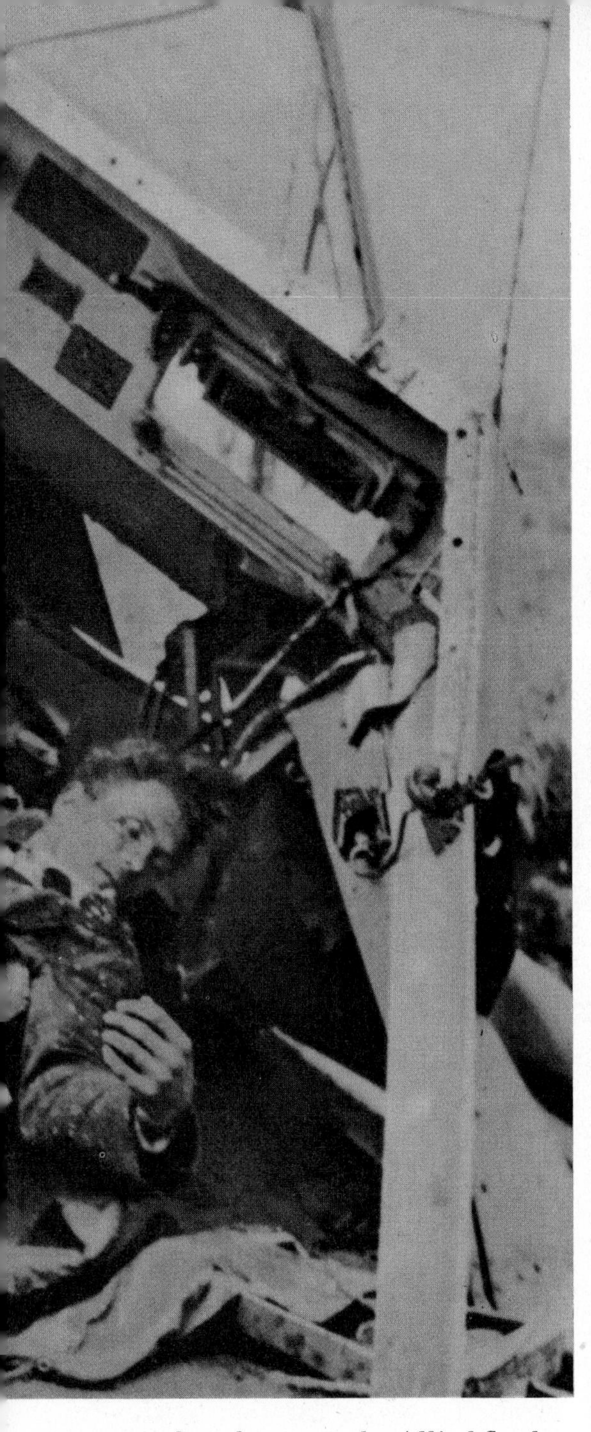

now an enclave between the Allied flanks. The little Dutch village of Roermond was still held by the German 15th Army, which formed the right of Army Group "B". On January 28, this rectifying operation, a prelude to the pincer attack called "Veritable/Grenade", was brought to a successful conclusion.

Rundstedt powerless

In this duel between Field-Marshal von Rundstedt and General Eisenhower, the former had at his disposal at the beginning of February (after he had lost the 6th *Panzerarmee,* taken away to help the Hungarian front), 73 divisions, including eight Panzer or *Panzergrenadier.* But the infantry divisions had fallen to an average of about 7,000 men each. As for the armoured formations, whatever may have been the excellent quality of their *matériel,* they suffered a continual shortage of petrol. In other words, as had started to become evident in the battle of Colmar, the crisis in munitions was getting ever more desperate at the front. The land forces of the Third Reich, moreover, could not rely on any support from the Luftwaffe, whose jet fighters were fully engaged attempting to defend what

Δ *Montgomery* (standing, right) *confers with Horrocks* (standing, left). *Note the insignia on the jeep: four stars, signifying that the owner was a general, and the badge of the 21st Army Group. This latter was a blue cross on a red shield, with two crossed golden swords superimposed.*

△ *As the Allies pushed on to the Rhine, the cities of Germany continued to suffer under the day and night efforts of the U.S. 8th and 15th Air Forces and R.A.F. Bomber Command. These are the gutted remains of Stuttgart.*

was left of Germany's cities against the redoubled attacks of the British and American Strategic Air Forces.

The last straw was that Rundstedt, in his office at Koblenz, was faced by a hopeless situation, and had been stripped of all initiative in the direction of operations. On January 21, he received the following incredible *Führerbefehl*, with orders to distribute it down to divisional level:

"Commanders-in-chief, army, corps, and divisional commanders are personally responsible to me for reporting in good time:

"*(a)* Every decision to execute an operational movement.

"*(b)* Every offensive plan from divisional level upwards that does not fit exactly with the directives of the higher command.

"*(c)* Every attack in a quiet sector intended to draw the enemy's attention to that sector, with the exception of normal shock troop actions.

"*(d)* Every plan for withdrawal or retreat.

"*(e)* Every intention of surrendering a position, a strongpoint, or a fortress.

"Commanders must make sure that I have time to intervene as I see fit, and that my orders can reach the front line troops in good time."

And the *Führer* further announced that any commander or staff officer who by "deliberate intent, carelessness, or oversight" hindered the execution of this order, would be punished with "draconian severity".

Allied superiority

From the Swiss frontier to the North Sea, Eisenhower had 70 divisions under his command on January 1, 1945:

	Infantry	*Armoured*	*Airborne*	*Total*
U.S.	31	11	3	45
British	7	4	1	12
Canadian	2	1	–	3
French	6	3	–	9
Polish	–	1	–	1
Totals	46	20	4	70

By May 8 this number would have been increased by another 15 American divisions (including four armoured), six French divisions, and two Canadian divisions (including one armoured).

Deducting six divisions fighting in the Alps or besieging German fortresses, this would give S.H.A.E.F. 87 divisions at the end of the war.

Despite the losses they had to bear, the

Allied divisions at this time were far less restricted than their German counterparts. The supply crisis, so acute in September, was now no more than an unpleasant memory. Petrol was in good supply and there was no shortage of shells at the front. The proximity fuses with which they were fitted allowed the gunners to fire shells which burst in the air, wreaking havoc among exposed troops. With reference to armour, the introduction into the United States Army of the heavy (41-ton) M26 General Pershing tank was significant. It was well-armoured, and had a 90-mm gun and good cross-country performance, the result of its Christie-type suspension and wide tracks. The Americans had rediscovered this suspension after seeing the results it gave in the service of the Germans, who had borrowed the idea from the Russians. The latter had acquired a licence to build the Christie suspension from the United States, after 1919, when the American military authorities had refused, in spite of the urging of the young Major George S. Patton, to take any firm interest in Christie and his advanced designs.

Thus the Allies' land forces were far more numerous than the Germans'. They also enjoyed powerful air support from a force which was both numerous and well-trained. Here General Devers had the Franco-American 1st Tactical Air Force (Major-General R. M. Webster), in which the French I Air Corps (Brigadier-General P. Gerardot) was itself attached to the French 1st Army. The United States 9th Air Force (Lieutenant-General Hoyt S. Vandenberg,) came under the overall command of General Bradley, and the British 2nd Tactical Air Force (Air-Marshal Sir Arthur Coningham) efficiently seconded Field-Marshal Montgomery's operations. On the German side there was nothing which could resist this formidable mass of flying artillery.

On November 12, 1944, 28 R.A.F. Lancasters attacked the great battleship *Tirpitz* in Tromsö with 12,000-lb "Tallboy" bombs and sank her at her anchorage. What was now left of the surface forces of the Kriegsmarine was being expended in the Baltic in attempts to help the army. As for the U-boats, which had lost 242 of their number during 1944, their successes in the North Atlantic between June 6, 1944 and May 8, 1945, were limited to the sinking of 31 merchant ships, displacing altogether only 178,000 tons. This was virtually nothing at all.

▵ An M26 General Pershing, the best American tank to see service in World War II. It was armed with a powerful 90-mm gun and was well armoured.

Complete surprise

At 0500 hours on February 8, 1,400 guns of the Canadian 1st Army blasted the German 84th Division, which had dug itself in along a seven-mile front between the Maas and the Waal close to the Dutch-German frontier. At 1030 hours, the British XXX Corps, which Montgomery had put under the command of General Crerar, moved in to the attack with five divisions (the British 51st, 53rd, and 15th and the Canadian 2nd and 3rd) in the first wave and the 43rd Division and the Guards Armoured Division in reserve. In all, according to the commander of the corps, Lieutenant-General Horrocks, there were 200,000 men and 35,000 vehicles.

The German position was heavily mined, and included a flooded area on the right and the thick Reichswald forest on the left. Moreover, the day before the attack, a thaw had softened the ground. Neither Hitler, at O.K.W., nor Colonel-General Blaskowitz, commanding Army Group "H", had been willing to accept the idea that Montgomery would choose such a sector in which to attack. Yet

General Schlemm, commanding the 1st Parachute Army, had warned them of this possibility. At the end of the day the 84th Division had lost 1,300 prisoners and was close to breaking-point.

Meanwhile the American 9th Army had been ordered to unleash Operation "Grenade" on February 10. This would cross the Rur and advance to the Rhine at Düsseldorf. Now came the flooding caused by the destruction of the Eifel dams, which held up the American 9th Army completely for 12 days and slowed down the British XXX Corps. The latter's units were also hopelessly mixed up. These delays allowed Schlemm to send his 7th and 6th Parachute, 15th *Panzergrenadier,* and then 116th Panzer Divisions to the rescue one after the other. And as Colonel C. P. Stacey, the official Canadian Army historian, notes, the Germans, at the edge of the abyss, had lost none of their morale:

"In this, the twilight of their gods, the defenders of the Reich displayed the recklessness of fanaticism and the courage of despair. In the contests west of the Rhine, in particular, they fought with special ferocity and resolution, rendering the battles in the Reichswald and Hochwald forests grimly memorable in the annals of this war."

On February 13, the Canadian 1st Army had mopped up the Reichswald and the little town of Kleve, and had reached Gennep, where it was reinforced across the Maas by the British 52nd Division and 11th Armoured Division. Schlemm threw two divisions of infantry into the battle as well as the famous Panzer-*"Lehr"* Division, and so the intervention of Lieutenant-General G. G. Simonds's Canadian II Corps at the side of the British XXX Corps did not have the decisive effect that Crerar expected. The 11th day of the offensive saw the attackers marking time on the Goch–Kalkar line about 15 miles from their jumping-off point.

▽ *The end of the* Tirpitz, *Germany's second and last battleship. Lying capsized in Tromsö fjord, with small vessels moored by her keel, she looks more like an island than a once-proud capital ship.*

But, just like the British 2nd Army in Normandy, the Canadian 1st Army had attracted the larger part of the enemy's forces, while the flood water in the Rur valley was going down. The weather also turned finer, and Montgomery fixed February 23 for the launching of Operation "Grenade". In his order of the day to the men of the 21st Army Group, Montgomery assured them that this was to be the beginning of the last round against Germany. The Third Reich was ready for the knock-out blow, which would be delivered from several directions.

Then, as an opening move, the Anglo-American Strategic Air Force launched 10,000 bombers and fighter-bombers and made the heaviest attack of the war on the Third Reich's communications network.

More than 200 targets featured on the programme of this attack, which went under the name of Operation "Clarion". Some of these objectives were bombed from only 4,500 feet because enemy anti-aircraft action was almost totally ineffective since Hitler had stripped it to supply the Eastern Front. The results of this bombing on February 22 were still noticeable when Colonel-General Jodl came to bring General Eisenhower the surrender of the Third Reich.

The following day, at 0245 hours, the artillery of the United States 9th Army opened fire on German positions on the Rur. The 15th Army (General von Zangen) which defended them, formed the right of Army Group "B" (Field-Marshal Model). Though it defended itself well, his 353rd Division was still thrown out of the ruins of Julich by the American XIX Corps (Major-General Raymond S. Maclain). Meanwhile, in the Linnich sector, XIII Corps (Major-General Alvan C. Gillem) had established a bridgehead a mile and a half deep. VII Corps (Lieutenant-General John L. Collins) of the American 1st Army, had also taken part in the attack and, by the end of the day, had mopped up Duren.

Hitler, Rundstedt, and Model used every last resource to tackle this new crisis looming on the horizon. Schlemm was stripped of the reinforcements which had just been despatched to him, and to these were added the 9th and 11th Panzer Divisions and the 3rd *Panzergrenadier* Division. These forces were instructed to hit the enemy's north-easterly push in its flank.

All the same, by February 27, the Allied breakthrough was complete near Erkelenz, and two days later, XIII Corps swept through the conurbation of Rheydt – Mönchengladbach. At the same time, to the right of the 9th Army, XVI Corps (Major-General J. B. Anderson) hurtled towards Roermond and Venlo behind the 1st Parachute Army, while on the right, XIX Corps was approaching Neuss opposite Düsseldorf.

In these circumstances Schlemm was ordered to retreat to the right bank of the Rhine, and he must be given all credit for carrying out this delicate and dangerous mission with remarkable skill. Rearguard skirmishes at Rheinberg, Sonsbeck, and Xanten gave him the time to get the bulk of his forces across and to complete the planned demolitions without fault. On March 6, the United States 9th Army and the Canadian 1st Army linked up opposite Wesel.

This joint Operation "Veritable/Grenade" cost the 18 German divisions

▵ The "Masters of the World" return home.

The British Hawker Tempest V Series 1 fighter and fighter-bomber

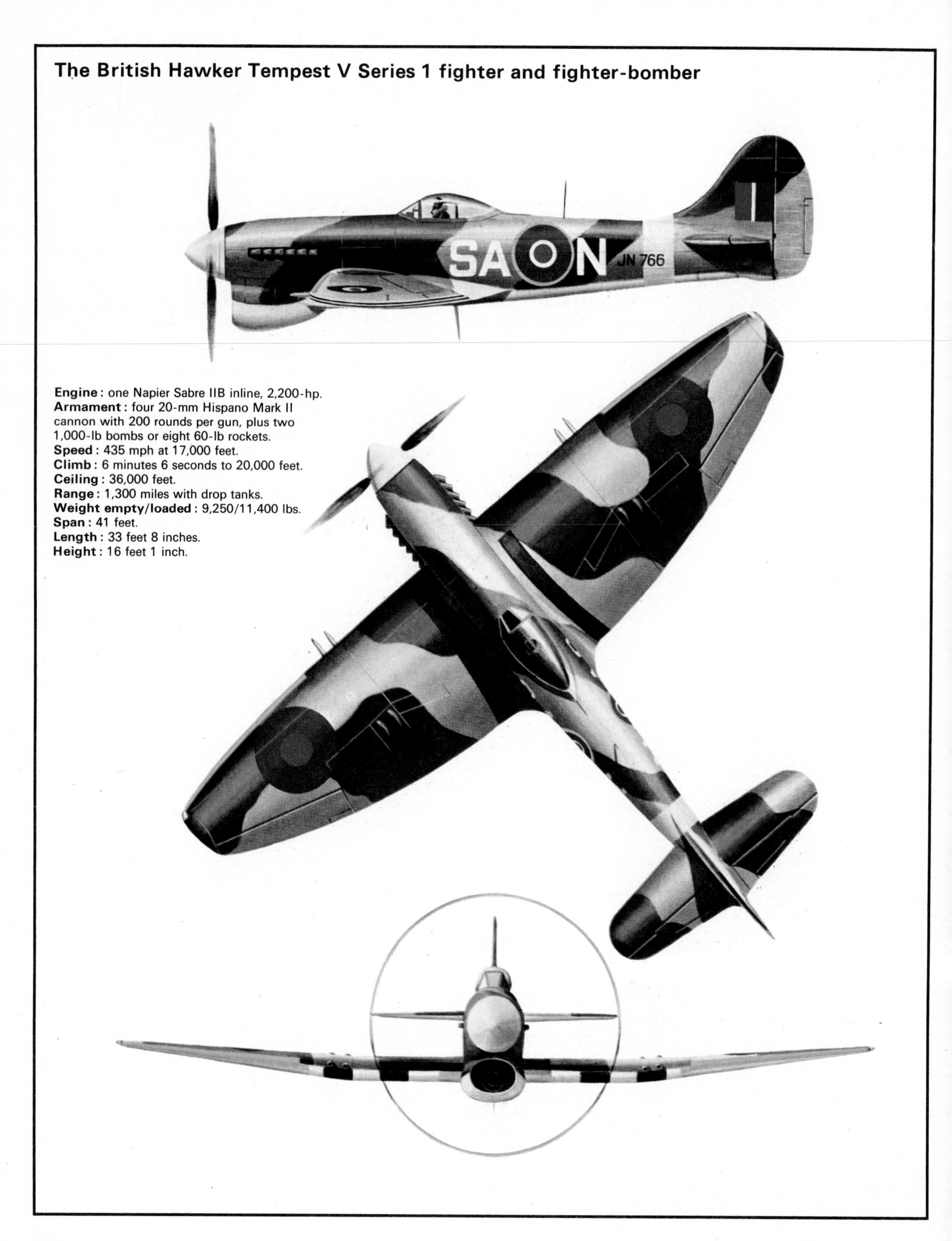

Engine: one Napier Sabre IIB inline, 2,200-hp.
Armament: four 20-mm Hispano Mark II cannon with 200 rounds per gun, plus two 1,000-lb bombs or eight 60-lb rockets.
Speed: 435 mph at 17,000 feet.
Climb: 6 minutes 6 seconds to 20,000 feet.
Ceiling: 36,000 feet.
Range: 1,300 miles with drop tanks.
Weight empty/loaded: 9,250/11,400 lbs.
Span: 41 feet.
Length: 33 feet 8 inches.
Height: 16 feet 1 inch.

engaged 53,000 prisoners. But Crerar alone had suffered 15,634 dead, wounded, and missing, of which 5,304 were Canadian troops.

On that same day, March 6, the leading division of the American VII Corps entered Cologne. Now the Allies were lining the Rhine between Cologne and Nijmegen, more than 100 miles downstream, where the river, if the stream slows down, widens to reach a breadth as great as 250 or 300 yards, and all the bridges had been destroyed. Forcing the Rhine north of the Ruhr, according to Montgomery's formula, would result in a delay of two weeks and necessitate considerable reinforcements for the 21st Army Group. And here can be seen Eisenhower's farsightedness in keeping to his plan of operations of December 31, 1944: to defeat the enemy west of the Rhine. For, if he had kept Bradley marking time then, Hitler could have detached the forces necessary to check Montgomery on the Rhine below Cologne.

This did not happen, for, on March 6, Army Group "B" was fighting the American 1st Army on its right and the 3rd on its centre. Its 5th *Panzerarmee* (Colonel-General Harpe) was now well and truly outflanked and overrun on both wings. According to the original plan, the American 1st Army was to provide the left flank of Operation "Grenade". With this in view, General Bradley had increased its size to three corps (14 divisions). But it was not foreseen that the 3rd Army would take part in the attack and it was only by a rather surreptitious move that, during the second week of January, Patton had pushed his forces as far as the Moselle in Luxembourg, the Sûre, and the Our near the *Westwall,* covering himself at S.H.A.E.F. by claiming that his moves were "offensive defence", when his aggression had no other aim but that of reaching the Rhine at Koblenz.

The defeat of the German 15th Army opened a breach in Field-Marshal Model's line which General Hodges and his 1st Army did not delay in exploiting. Having occupied Cologne, VII Corps set off for Bonn on March 7. III Corps (Major-General J. Millikin), which was advancing on the right of VII Corps, had orders to take the crossings over the Ahr. This task was entrusted to the 9th Armoured Division (Major-General John W. Leonard).

Towards the end of the morning of March 7, Brigadier-General William M. Hoge, leading Combat Command "B" of the 9th Armoured Division, was informed that the Ludendorff Bridge near Remagen was still intact. He decided not to follow his orders (which had specified Sinzig as his target) to the letter and resolved there and then to chance his luck and seize the bridge. A little before 1600 hours, 2nd Lieutenant Karl Timmermann ventured on to the bridge, followed by the Burrows section. Seeing them, the German guard tried to set off the demolition charges, but in vain. Under American fire, Sergeant Faust, another hero of this episode, then lit the fuse. But the effect of the explosion was insignificant, and, a few minutes later, Sergeant Alex Drabik was the first American fighting man to step on the right bank of the Rhine. Behind him, Lieutenant Hugh B. Mott, a combat engineer, and three sappers tore the charges from the girders and threw the explosives into the river.

"The enemy had reached Kreuzberg and as far as a bridge near Remagen which, it appears, was encumbered with fugitives. They crossed the bridge and succeeded in forming a bridgehead on the eastern bank of the river. Counter-attack early this morning. The 11th Panzer Division will be brought from Bonn. But petrol is in short supply."

The O.K.W. war diary records this national catastrophe in these unemotional words. Therefore it gives no account of Hitler's rage, which was terrible. Major Scheler and three others were declared responsible, on Hitler's orders, for the success of the Allied surprise attack, court-martialled, and shot.

Twenty-four hours after this surprise, there were already 8,000 Americans in the bridgehead. By March 17, four divisions (9th, 78th, 99th, and 9th Armoured) were dug in. On the same day the bridge collapsed. Hitler had concentrated the fire of a battery of 17-cm guns on it, as well as ordering aircraft and V-2 attacks, and even attempts by Kriegsmarine human torpedoes and frogmen. But, protected by booms and nets, 1st Army engineers had already built another bridge and both banks of the Rhine were bristling with anti-aircraft guns.

Having transferred III Corps (three divisions) to the 1st Army, Patton remained in command of VIII, XII, and XX Corps, which had 12 divisions, three of which were armoured. The crossing of the Our and the Sûre, on the Saint Vith–Echternach line, was no little matter because

▵ *The nemesis of Germany's civilian bombing campaigns early in the war: the avenging angel of the British and American strategic bombing forces.*

the rivers were in flood. The forcing of *Westwall* was also very tough. In XII Corps there was one division which had to reduce 120 concrete casemates. This it did with self-propelled 155-mm guns, pounding the embrasures from a range of only 300 yards.

In spite of everything, by the end of February VIII and XII Corps were on the Kyll, having advanced about 20 miles into German territory. XX Corps had taken Saarburg and advanced as far as the apex of the triangle formed by the Mosel and the Saar at their confluence a little above Trier. Up till then the German 7th Army (General Brandenberger), which faced Patton, had defended itself tenaciously, but this very tenacity explains why, on March 1, having exhausted its supplies, it literally collapsed. On that day, wrote Patton:

"At 14.15, Walker [commander of XX Corps] called up to say the 10th Armoured Division was in Trier and had captured a bridge over the Moselle intact. The capture of this bridge was due to the heroic act of Lieutenant Colonel J. J. Richardson, deceased. He was riding in the leading vehicle of his battalion of armoured infantry when he saw the wires leading to the demolition charges at the far end of the bridge. Jumping out of the vehicle, he raced across the bridge under heavy fire and cut the wires. The acid test of battle brings out the pure metal."

ΔΔ *The last stand . . .*
Δ *. . . and the last* Heil.

On March 3, the forcing of the Kyll at Kyllburg by the 5th Division, under Major-General S. LeRoy Irwin, enabled Major-General Manton Eddy, commanding XII Corps, to detach his 4th Division. Under the command of Major-General Hugh J. Gaffey, this division made a raid of mad audacity, covering 26 miles on March 4 alone and reaching Daun in the evening. Two days later, it reached the Rhine above Koblenz. On its left, the 11th Armoured Division (Major-General Holmes E. Dager), advancing ahead of VII Corps, established first contact with the American 1st Army on March 11, near Brohl.

On March 8, the O.K.W. war diary noted that LIII Corps had been steamrollered and that any co-ordinated conduct of operations was henceforth impossible. The truth of this is illustrated by the capture of General von Rothkirch und Panthen, in command of LIII Corps. Bradley recounts the story thus:

"So rapid was the dissolution that even the senior German commanders lost touch with their crumbling front. One day a German corps commander drove into a field of listless soldiers and asked why they were not fighting the Allies. Not until an American MP clasped him on the shoulder and invited him to join the throng, did the general learn that he had stumbled into a PW concentration."

Altogether, the second phase of the battle for the Rhineland, called Operation "Lumberjack", had brought the 12th Army Group 51,000 prisoners. It had also given it the priceless bridgehead at Remagen, which the German 15th Army was unable to destroy, since the four Panzer divisions which Model had given

△ *A German soldier lies dead on the bank of the Rhine, the Third Reich's "uncrossable" natural defence in the West.*

the energetic Lieutenant-General Bayerlein for this purpose did not total more than 5,000 men, 60 tanks, and 30 guns. On the other side of the battlefield, the Americans spread out in all directions. So great and thorough was their push that, on March 22, they were on the right bank of the Rhine in a bridgehead 25 miles long and ten miles deep.

No retreat

As explained earlier, because of the forces and *matériel* requested by Montgomery in order to lead his army group across the Rhine to the north of the Ruhr, Eisenhower had at first limited his operation to the left bank of the Mosel. However, Hitler's obstinate decision to keep his Army Group "G" inside the salient limited by Haguenau, Saarbrücken, Cochem (north of the Mosel), and Koblenz, would convince him that the best thing to do was to strike a third blow at the enemy on the west of the Rhine, which meant that the 3rd Army and the 6th Army Group would be able to take part.

Colonel-General Hausser, commanding Army Group "G", had just been given

Δ *An American artillery column streams past the wreckage of a German convoy blasted by the Allies' heavy guns.*

the 7th Army, recently taken over by General Obstfelder, and which was at present heavily engaged against Patton.

Hausser still had the 1st Army (General Foertsch), which was occupying the Moder front and the Siegfried Line or *Westwall* as far as the approaches to Forbach. The 19th Army, having evacuated the Colmar pocket, now came directly under the command of O.K.W. But at this time all these units totalled only 13 divisions, most of them badly worn, though some of them still gave a good account of themselves, for example the 2nd Mountain Division (Lieutenant-General Degen), and the 6th S.S. Mountain Division (Lieutenant-General Brenner).

Under these conditions, Hausser and his army commanders were of the opinion that they ought to put the Rhine, between the junctures of the Mosel and the Lauter, behind them as soon as possible and be ready to abandon the Siegfried Line after having destroyed all its installations. But Hitler reacted indignantly to this suggestion of destroying a masterpiece of German military engineering to which he had contributed so much.

The Führer was mistaken about the value of this construction, however. Patton, who visited one of the fortresses taken by the 76th Division, points out its weak point with his usual perspicacity:

"It consisted of a three storey submerged barracks with toilets, shower baths, a hospital, laundry, kitchen, store rooms and every conceivable convenience plus an enormous telephone installation. Electricity and heat were produced by a pair of identical diesel engines with generators. Yet the whole offensive capacity of this installation consisted of two machine guns and a 60-mm mortar operating from steel cupolas which worked up and down by means of hydraulic lifts. The 60-mm mortar was peculiar in that it was operated by remote control. As in all cases, this particular pill box was taken by a dynamite charge against the back door. We found marks on the cupolas, which were ten inches thick, where our 90-mm shells fired at a range of two hundred yards, had simply bounced."

But neither Hitler nor his subordinates imagined that Patton would need only four or five days to shift the centre of gravity of his 3rd Army from Brohl and Koblenz on the Rhine to Mayen on the Nette and Cochem on the Mosel. On the left, VIII Corps, now reduced to two divisions, would keep watch on Koblenz. In the centre, XII Corps, increased to six divisions (5th, 76th, 89th, and 90th Infantry, and 4th and 11th Armoured), was given Bingen on the Rhine and Bad-Kreuznach on the Nahe as its first targets. On the right, XX Corps with four divisions (26th, 80th, and 94th Infantry and 10th Armoured) had orders to press on to Kaiserslautern behind the backs of the defenders of the *Westwall,* which would be attacked frontally by the American 7th Army. The latter, commanded by Lieutenant-General Alexander M. Patch, had 12 divisions, including the 3rd Algerian Division. As can be seen, the third act of the Battle of the Rhine, named "Undertone" was about to match 22 more or less intact Allied divisions against 13 worn-out German ones. Actually, since the end of January, the 7th Army had been waiting poised between Haguenau and Forbach.

As for the 3rd Army, its losses, between January 29 and March 12, amounted to only 21,581 officers, N.C.O.s, and men, of which 3,650 had been killed and 1,374 were missing, which gives a daily divisional average of eight killed or missing and 32 wounded. These figures would suggest that despite his nickname of "Blood and Guts", Patton was not at all prodigal with the lives of his men.

Triumphant advance

On the evening of March 14, XII Corps had already got most of its 5th and 90th Divisions over on the right bank of the Mosel at Treis, eight miles below Cochem. Eddy then wasted no time in unleashing his 4th and 11th Armoured Divisions.

To his right, XX Corps was attacking towards Saint Wendel, in the rear of the *Westwall.* At last, at dawn on March 15, H-hour came for the 7th Army. Its VI Corps (3rd Algerian, 36th, 42nd, and 103rd Divisions and 14th Armoured Division), went into the attack on the Moder front. Its 15th Division attacked the *Westwall,* its left towards Saarlautern, the French Sarrelouis, in contact with XX Corps.

By March 16, the 4th Armoured Division had advanced 32 miles in 48 hours. As it crossed the Nahe, near Bad-Kreuznach, it clashed violently with the 2nd Panzer Division (Major-General von Lauchert). But Patton was aware of the audacity of Gaffey, his ex-chief-of-staff, and had not let him fight it out alone. Opportunely reinforced, the 4th Armoured Division defeated the desperate counter-attack and moved forward again. By March 19, it had arrived seven miles west of Worms and 12 miles south-west of Mainz. On the same day, XX Corps, to which the 7th Army had given the 12th Armoured Division, under Major-General R. R. Allen, pushed its armoured spearheads as far as 15 miles from Kaiserslautern. Since the crossing of the Mosel, the 3rd Army had lost, including accidents, only 800 men, while it had taken 12,000 prisoners.

Forty-eight hours later, in XII Corps, the 90th Division, which had lost two commanders in Normandy, was busy mopping up Mainz, the 4th Armoured Division was occupying Worms, and the 11th was pushing on to the south of the city.

In XX Corps, Major-General Walton H. Walker had thrown his 12th Armoured Division into Ludwigshafen and was pushing his 10th towards Landau. Just as the difficult terrain of the Eifel had been no impediment, that of the Hunsruck, which is just as bad, had not been able to hold back the *élan* of the 3rd Army, supported flexibly and efficiently by Major-General Otto P. Weyland's XIX Tactical Air Command of the 9th Air Force.

Facing the German 1st Army, the American 7th Army had had a considerably more difficult task. There is some evidence of this in a note made by Pierre Lyautey who, as liaison officer, was with the 3rd Algerian Division (General

Δ General Sir Miles Dempsey, commander of the British 2nd Army, on an inspection tour of his front line units.

∆ *An American quadruple .5-inch A.A. mounting on a half-track chassis on watch against German aircraft near the Château de Vianden in Luxembourg.*

Guillaume), when it attacked across the Moder.

"March 15: Artillery preparation. The planned 2,000 shells light up the scene. Attack by the 4th Tunisians. Skirmishes. The leading company runs, at seven in the morning, from ruin to ruin, lonely wall to lonely wall, reaches the railway, dives into the underground passage and jumps up into the mangled and dismantled gasworks. Violent reaction from German artillery, mortar, and machine guns. Impossible to move out. The whole sector is alive with fire. The company shelters in the gas-works. First one tank explodes, then another. Beyond the church, the scene is one of a major offensive: stretcher-bearers, stretchers, limping men walking around with white cards, a smell of blood, stifling heat. The last cows of Oberhoffen-Bénarès are in their death agony among the rubble."

It took four days for Major-General Edward H. Brooks, commanding VI Corps, to take back from the Germans the ground lost in lower Alsace as a result of Operation *"Nordwind"*. Then he closed in on the *Westwall* between the Rhine and the Vosges.

Both General de Gaulle and General de Lattre had no intention, however, of allowing the French Army to be restricted to a purely defensive function on the left bank of the Rhine. They wanted to see it play a part in the invasion of the Third Reich. While awaiting a definite decision from S.H.A.E.F., General de Gaulle writes, "General Devers, a good ally and a good friend, sympathised with de Lattre's wishes".

That is why, on March 18, General de Monsabert received command of a task force comprising the 3rd Algerian Division and two-thirds of the 5th Armoured Division; aiming for Speyer, it would give the French 1st Army a front over the Rhine in Germany.

The three infantry divisions of the United States VI Corps took three days and lost 2,200 men to overcome that part of the *Westwall* allotted to them as objective, but using its infantry and engineers

△ *The great prize. Men and vehicles of the American 1st Army pour across the Ludendorff railway bridge over the Rhine at Remagen to establish an invincible bridgehead on the right bank.*

in turn, Brooks finally pierced the defences between Wissembourg and Pirmasens. As for Monsabert, he had difficulty in front of the Bienwald. Nevertheless, his tanks were around Maximiliansau opposite Karlsruhe by the evening of March 24.

Patch had taken Landau the day before, so the Battle of the Palatinate, the third act of the Battle of the Rhine, was drawing to its end.

The battle had been conducted to Eisenhower's complete satisfaction. Between February 8 and March 24, the enemy had lost 280,000 prisoners, the remains of five German armies which had crossed back over the Rhine between the German-Dutch and Franco-German frontiers. Army Group "B" had suffered most. Patton alone could claim 140,112 prisoners, against the 53,000 taken by the 21st Army Group in Operation "Veritable/ Grenade". Therefore Eisenhower had proved his superiority not only over Hitler's arms but also over Montgomery's arguments.

Furthermore, on the night of March 22/23, Patton also succeeded in crossing the Rhine as Bradley had recommended, profiting from the Germans' disorder. The banks there being suitable, Patton chose the stretch near Oppenheim, which

▵▵ *A Sherman of the U.S. Army is ferried across a river on a section of pontoon bridge pushed by motor-boats.*
▹ *The Allies advance to the Rhine, and the establishment of the first bridgeheads at Remagen and Oppenheim.*

was occupied by the 5th Division (Major-General S. LeRoy Irwin), half-way between Worms and Mainz.

Surprise crossing

At 2230 hours, 200 Piper L-4 Grasshoppers began to shuttle from one bank to the other. These small observation and artillery-spotting aircraft carried an armed infantryman instead of an observer. Once the first bridgehead had thus been formed, the 12 L.C.V.P.s (Landing Craft Vehicle/Personnel) of the "naval detachment" which Patton had trained to a high pitch of efficiency on the Moselle at Toul, entered the river while his bridging crews, from which he had refused to be separated (lest he not get them back) when he had driven hard from the Sarre to the Ardennes, began to work at once under the command of Brigadier-General Conklin, the 3rd Army's chief engineer.

At dawn on March 23, the 5th Division had already placed six infantry battalions, about 4,000 or 5,000 men, on the right bank of the Rhine, at the cost of only eight killed and 20 wounded. The Germans were so surprised that when Patton made his report to Bradley, he asked him not to publicise the news, so as to keep the Germans in the dark while they expected him at the approaches to Mainz. As an all-American soldier, he was happy to have stolen a march over "Monty" by forcing the Rhine before him and without making any demands on anybody.

As a result, 48 hours later, five divisions of the 3rd Army had crossed the Rhine at Oppenheim, stretched along the valley of the Main: XII Corps towards Aschaffenburg, and XX Corps towards Hanau.

CHAPTER 147

Across the Rhine

On March 8, 1945, Field-Marshal Kesselring was ordered to leave the Italian theatre of operations immediately and go to an audience with the *Führer*. The following afternoon, Hitler told him that as a result of the unfortunate situation at Remagen, he had decided to make him Commander-in-Chief in the West. In his account of the meeting, Kesselring writes:

"Without attaching any blame to Rundstedt, Hitler justified his action with the argument that a younger and more flexible leader, with greater experience of fighting the Western powers, and still possessing the troops' full confidence, could perhaps make himself master of the situation in the West. He was aware of the inherent difficulties of assuming command at such a juncture, but there

▽ *The Americans cross the Rhine: an M24 Chaffee light tank prepares to reverse into a landing craft on the west bank prior to going across, while other landing craft shuttle to and fro in the background and B-24 Liberator bombers head east to disrupt German communications further.*

△ *Trucks fitted with special jigs move pontoons up towards the west bank of the Rhine in preparation for the American 9th Army's crossing.*

was no alternative but for me to make this sacrifice in spite of the poor state of my health. He had full confidence in me and expected me to do all that was humanly possible."

Such was the conclusion of the general review of the situation that Hitler had spent several hours discussing with Kesselring, first alone, later in the company of Keitel and Jodl. On the whole, Hitler was optimistic about the future. One might have suspected him of trying to mislead Kesselring as to the true situation were it not for his own unique capacity for self-deception. In any event, he appeared satisfied with the course of events on the Eastern Front.

Hitler certainly thought that a collapse in the East would be the end of the war, but he had provided for this eventuality and added, according to Kesselring's notes taken immediately after the audience: "our main military effort is directed to the East. He [Hitler] envisages the decisive battle there, with complete confidence. And he expects the enemy's main attack to be launched at Berlin."

For this reason the 9th Army, which was charged with the defence of the city, had been given priority consideration. Under the command of General T. Busse, it had:

1. adequate infantry strength, together with Panzer and anti-tank forces;
2. standard artillery strength and more than adequate anti-aircraft defences, deployed in considerable depth under the best artillery commanders available;
3. excellent positions, with the best of defences, especially water barriers, on both sides of the main battle line; and
4. in its rear the strongest position of all, Berlin, with its fortified perimeter and whole defensive organisation.

So there were grounds for assurance that the Berlin front would not be broken; similarly with Army Group "Centre", on the borders of Silesia and Czechoslovakia, which had gained notable successes. Its commander, Schörner, assured Hitler that "with reinforcements and sufficient supplies, he would repel all enemy attacks launched at him".

As regards the situation on the Western Front, the heavy losses sustained by the British, Americans, and French over months of heavy fighting were a factor that should be taken into account. Furthermore, in Hitler's opinion, "the Allies could not dismiss the natural obstacles covering the German Army's positions. The Allied bridgehead at Remagen was the danger point and it was urgent it should be mopped up; but there too Hitler was confident."

In these conditions, Kesselring's task was to hold on long enough for the Eastern Front armies to be brought up to strength, so that O.K.W. could then despatch the necessary reinforcements to the armies in the West. Within a short while, the deficiencies of the Luftwaffe, held to blame for the failures of recent months, would be forgotten and Grand-Admiral Dönitz's new submarines would have turned the tables in the Battle of the Atlantic, bringing much needed relief to the defence of the Third Reich.

Kesselring caught off balance

Thus armed with encouragement, Kesselring received his chief-of-staff's report in the night of March 9-10 at the H.Q. at Ziegenberg just vacated by Rundstedt. General Westphal had been his chief-of-

▵ Waiting for the big day: Allied supplies under camouflage by the side of a road leading to the Rhine and the heart of Germany.

The Canadian Ram Kangaroo armoured personnel carrier

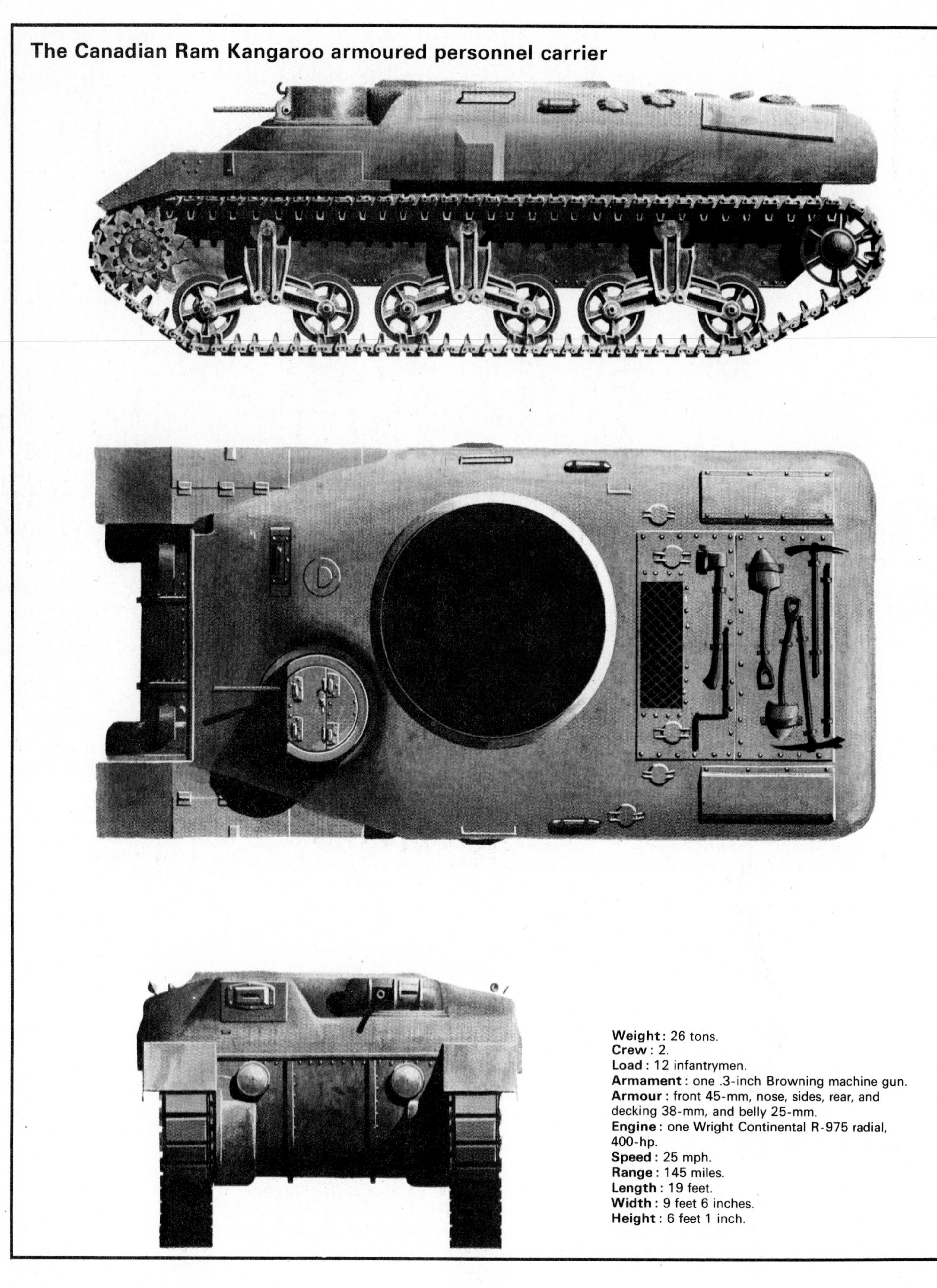

Weight: 26 tons.
Crew: 2.
Load: 12 infantrymen.
Armament: one .3-inch Browning machine gun.
Armour: front 45-mm, nose, sides, rear, and decking 38-mm, and belly 25-mm.
Engine: one Wright Continental R-975 radial, 400-hp.
Speed: 25 mph.
Range: 145 miles.
Length: 19 feet.
Width: 9 feet 6 inches.
Height: 6 feet 1 inch.

△ *Men of the Cheshire Regiment prepare to board the Landing Vehicles Tracked that will ferry them over the Rhine in the afternoon of March 24. At 2200 hours the previous night, the 1st Commando Brigade had made an assault landing on the east bank and secured the bridgehead into which the Cheshire Regiment moved as reinforcements.*
Overleaf: *White phosphorus shells from the U.S. 3rd Army's artillery rain down on the slopes above a small Rhenish town.*

staff during his time as supreme commander in Italy, and Kesselring had complete confidence in him.

The new commander must have been considerably shocked by the unembroidered account of the situation that he received. With 55 battle-worn divisions giving him, on average, a coverage of 63 fighting men for each mile of the front, it was his task to hold 85 full strength Allied divisions, which also enjoyed all the benefits of undisputed air superiority.

On March 11, at the H.Q. of LIII Corps, Kesselring met Field-Marshal Model and General von Zangen, commanding the 15th Army, which had been given the job of wiping out the Remagen bridgehead. All were agreed that this objective could not be attained unless there was considerable speeding up in the supply of substantial reinforcements, and above all of ammunition, and this filled Kesselring with apprehension. The morale of Army Group "H" gave him some comfort, however, especially since the enemy attack across the lower Rhine was taking time in getting under way. On the other hand, the position of Army Group "G", without any mobile reserves worthy of the name, seemed fraught with risk.

Hence Kesselring was not so much caught unawares as off guard by Operation "Undertone", which he learnt had been launched when he returned from this rapid tour of inspection. The cadence given the attack by Patton, Walker, Eddy, and their excellent divisional commanders was a disagreeable revelation to the Germans; Kesselring wrote:

"What clearly emerged was the rapid succession of operations (showing that the Allies had abandoned their Italian campaign strategy) as well as the competency of command and the almost reckless engagement of armoured units in terrain that was quite unsuited for the use of heavy tanks. On the basis of my experience in Italy in similar terrain, I was not expecting the American armoured forces to achieve rapid success, in spite of the fact that the reduced strength of tired German troops gave undoubted advantage to the enemy operation."

In the face of this violent American thrust, O.B. West appealed to O.K.W. for authorisation to withdraw the German 1st and 7th Armies to the right bank of the Rhine; typically, Hitler procrastinated until it was too late to accept this eminently reasonable course. And the only reinforcement destined for the Western Front was a single division, which was not even combat-worthy as it had spent some considerable time in Denmark on garrison duties. To cap this, Kesselring was informed of the surprise attack at Oppenheim, while the 1st Parachute Army brought news that north of the Ruhr, smokescreens maintained over several hours showed that Montgomery was putting the final touches to his careful preparations.

To surrender or not?

It was in these circumstances that Kesselring was contacted by *Obergruppenführer* Karl Wolff of the *Waffen*-S.S., whom he had known in the capacity of "Plenipotentiary for the Wehrmacht in the rear of the Italian Front". For the past few weeks, this officer had been engaged, via Major Waibel of Swiss Army Intelligence, in negotiation with Allen Dulles, head of the American Secret Services in Berne, about terms for the capitulation of the German forces fighting in Italy. On March 23, Kesselring, who knew what Wolff was up to, saw him in his office in Ziegenberg, where Wolff suggested directly that the German armies in the West should be associated with this bid for surrender.

Kesselring refused, in spite of the succession of telephone calls informing him of the rapid progress made by the Americans, who had broken out of the Oppenheim bridgehead. According to Wolff's report to Dulles, Kesselring's opposition was based on both moral and practical arguments:

"He was defending soil and he was bound to continue even if he died himself in the fighting. He said he personally owed everything to the Führer, his rank, his appointment, his decorations. To this he added that he hardly knew the generals commanding the corps and divisions under him. Moreover, he had a couple of well-armed S.S. divisions behind him which he was certain would take action against him if he undertook anything

Field-Marshal Albrecht von Kesselring was born in Bavaria in 1885. He served as a staff officer in the artillery throughout World War I and the 1920's, and in 1933 he was transferred to the air force. He commanded the Luftwaffe in the German invasion of Poland and Belgium, and ordered the bombing of the B.E.F. as it evacuated Dunkirk. He conducted the extremely successful bombing raids on R.A.F. bases in southern England in 1940 and in July of that year he was made a Field-Marshal. In 1941 he was appointed C.-in-C., South, sharing with Rommel the command of the North African campaign and taking over during Rommel's absence and later during the retreat from Tunisia. In 1943 he was C.-in-C. in Italy, conducting a brilliant campaign despite the indifference of his superiors to his constant pleas for air reinforcements. For over a year he held out against the Allied advance, with a superbly conceived line of defences behind Cassino. In 1945 he succeeded the cream of Hitler's generals on the Western Front in a desperate attempt to check the Allied advance, but in March he had to surrender the southern half of the German forces to the Allies. He was sentenced to death by a British military court for executing Italian hostages, but in 1947 his sentence was commuted to life imprisonment and in 1952 he was released on the grounds of ill health. He died in 1960.

▷ *American paratroops dig in under the trees of a German orchard after the airborne landings just to the east of the Allied bridgeheads over the Rhine. The Germans, who had expected landings much further behind their lines, were caught entirely on the wrong foot by the Allied use of airborne troops in a tactical rather than a strategic rôle.*

▽ *The parachute drops begin in the Wesel area. This photograph was taken by Sergeant Fred W. Quandt of San Francisco, California, from a B-17 camera plane. The B-17 was shot down a few minutes later–the first aircraft casualty of the operation.*

The British General Aircraft Hamilcar I glider

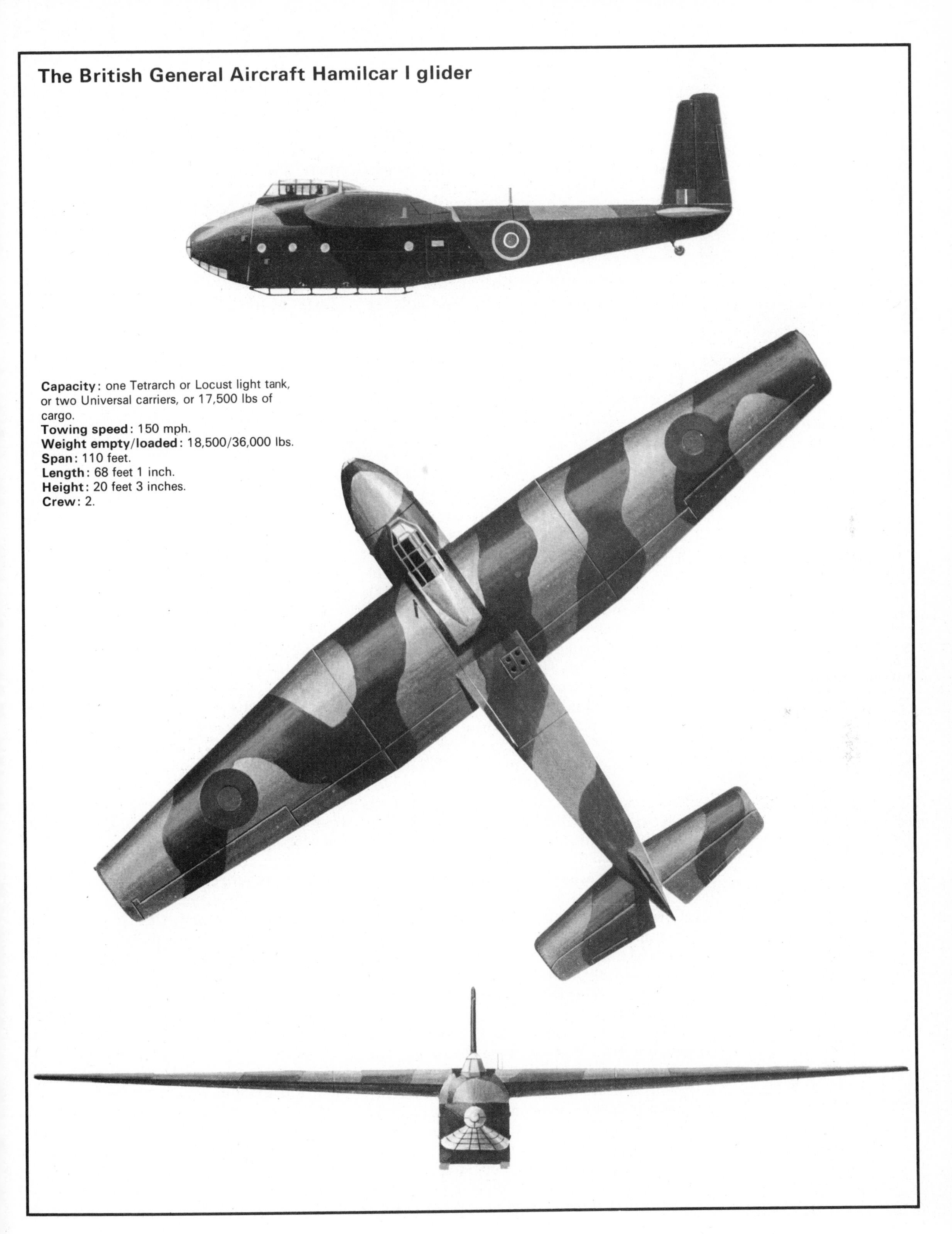

Capacity: one Tetrarch or Locust light tank, or two Universal carriers, or 17,500 lbs of cargo.
Towing speed: 150 mph.
Weight empty/loaded: 18,500/36,000 lbs.
Span: 110 feet.
Length: 68 feet 1 inch.
Height: 20 feet 3 inches.
Crew: 2.

▵ *A German N.C.O. illustrates how to fire a* Panzerfaust *30m anti-tank rocket projector. There were four* Panzerfaust *models, all working the same way: the rocket was contained in a tube held under the arm or over the shoulder. When fired, the rocket motor drove the weapon out of the tube and on towards the target. Just as the weapon left the tube, a cap at the latter's rear was pushed off, allowing the exhaust to fan out to the rear. The warhead of the rocket was a hollow-charge device containing 3 pounds 7½ ounces of explosive, capable of penetrating 200 mm of armour sloped at 30 degrees. It was an extremely efficient weapon, with a punch equal to that of the dual-purpose 8.8-cm gun.*

▵▹ *German prisoners are escorted through the town of Hamminkeln by their captors, men of the British 6th Airborne Division.*

▿▹ *German civilians and prisoners hug the ground in the courtyard of a captured farmhouse in an effort to protect themselves from retaliatory German artillery fire.*

against the Führer's orders."

Nevertheless Kesselring had no objection to a German capitulation in Italy, and the *Obergruppenführer* was quite free to convey to the former's successor, Colonel-General von Vietinghoff, that O.B. West entirely approved the project.

Scorched earth policy

Whatever one may think of the ethical considerations behind Kesselring's refusal, he understandably felt no scruples in giving his support to Albert Speer, Reich Minister for Armaments and War Production, who was doing all he could to sabotage the execution of the "scorched earth" order promulgated by Hitler on March 19, 1945.

In setting out its motives, the monstrous *Führerbefehl* used the following line of argument:

"The fight for the existence of our people obliges us to make total use, even within the Reich, of whatever means may weaken the fighting power of the enemy and prevent him from pursuing his advance. Any means capable, directly or indirectly, of inflicting lasting damage on the offensive strength of the enemy must be resorted to. It is erroneous to think that by leaving them intact or with only superficial damage, we may more profitably resume exploitation of our communication and transport systems and our industrial or productive installations when we reconquer our invaded territory. When the enemy comes to retreat, he will have no consideration for the population, and will leave only scorched earth behind him.

"For this reason I command:

1. that within the Reich the communications and military transport systems, and the industrial and productive installations, which the enemy may use immediately or within a limited period for the prosecution of the war, be destroyed."

Article 2 of the same decree divided powers for this purpose between the military chiefs and the civil administrators; and Article 3, ordering the immediate transmission of the order to army commanders, declared invalid any directive which sought to nullify it.

So Hitler joined Morgenthau, whereas even Churchill and Roosevelt had rejected the inhuman and demented notion of "pastoralising" the German people. Albert Speer, however, devoted his entire energies to opposing the implementation of this insane order: verbally on March 18; and in writing in two letters, the second of which, dated March 29, is preserved among the appendices that Percy Ernst Schramm adds as a supplement to his masterly edition of the O.K.W. war diary. The extract chosen below is evidence enough for the reader that the motives which inspired Hitler on this occasion were essentially the same as those of the Scythian kings who, on their deathbeds, according to Herodotus, caused their favourite wives, their servants, and even their horses to be sacrificed. And, Speer wrote:

"From what you have told me this evening [March 18] the following emerges clearly and unequivocally, unless I have misunderstood you: if we are to lose the war, the German people are to be lost as well. This destiny is unavoidable. This being so, it is not necessary to secure the basic conditions to enable our people to ensure their own survival even in the most primitive form. Rather, on the contrary, we should ourselves destroy them. For they will have proved themselves the weaker, and the future will belong exclusively to the people of the east, who will have shown themselves the stronger. Furthermore, only the unworthy will survive since the best and bravest will have fallen."

Speer did not limit his opposition merely to pious utterances. He put the enormous weight of influence he had as dictator of industrial production to the task of avoiding implementation of the "scorched earth" order.

In this covert activity he received positive support from Kesselring; as a result, in its retreat from the Rhine to the Elbe and beyond, the German Army restricted itself to forms of destruction which are common in such cases to all the armies in the world. Two circumstances favoured Speer in carrying out his policy: the headlong nature of the Allied advance after March 31 and, in the German camp, the explosives crisis, further exacerbated by the disorganisation of transport.

At the end of 1966, on his release from Spandau prison, to which he had been sent by the Nuremberg trial, Albert Speer was greeted by manifestations of sympathy. This was interpreted by some as the sign they had been seeking since

1945 of a recrudescence of Nazism in the Federal Republic. Such an interpretation seems quite unwarranted. Rather, it would seem that Speer's sympathisers wanted to show public recognition of the man who, in spite of Hitler and at the risk of his life, had chosen to safeguard the means of survival and recovery so that one day another Germany might live.

Montgomery prepares to cross the Rhine

On March 23, at 1530 hours, under a clear sky and with a favourable weather forecast, Montgomery launched Operation "Plunder/Varsity" and addressed the American, British, and Canadian troops under his command with an order of the day which concluded with these words: "6. 21 ARMY GROUP WILL NOW

The American Landing Vehicle Tracked (L.V.T.) 2 Buffalo

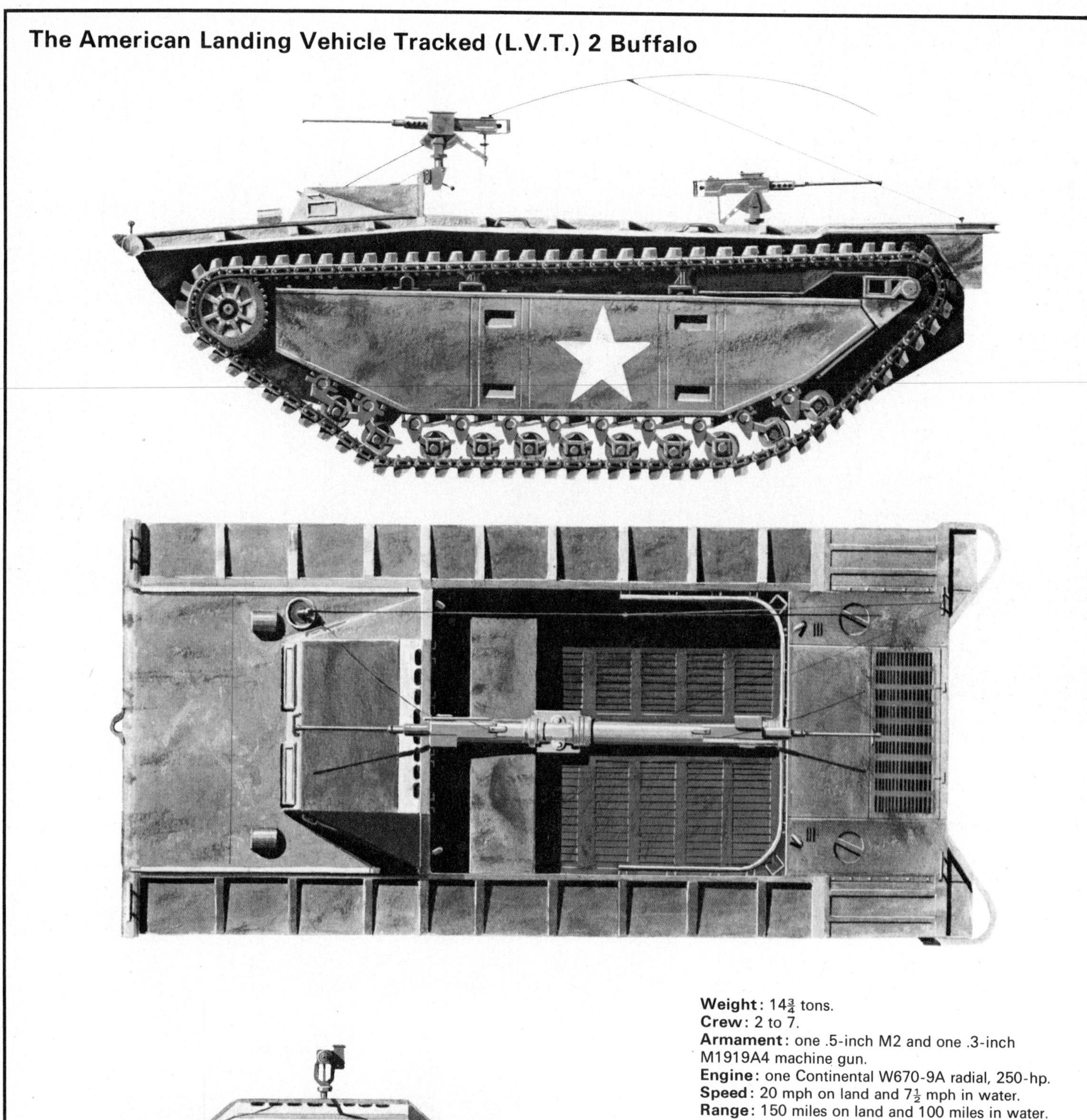

Weight: $14\frac{3}{4}$ tons.
Crew: 2 to 7.
Armament: one .5-inch M2 and one .3-inch M1919A4 machine gun.
Engine: one Continental W670-9A radial, 250-hp.
Speed: 20 mph on land and $7\frac{1}{2}$ mph in water.
Range: 150 miles on land and 100 miles in water.
Length: 26 feet 2 inches.
Width: 10 feet 8 inches.
Height: 8 feet $2\frac{1}{2}$ inches.

△ *A battery of British 40-mm Bofors guns in action in the direct support rôle.*
Overleaf: *An American Landing Vehicle Tracked (L.V.T.) splashes into the Rhine under cover of a thick smokescreen.*

CROSS THE RHINE
The enemy possibly thinks he is safe behind this great river obstacle. We all agree that it is a great obstacle; but we will show the enemy that he is far from safe behind it. This great Allied fighting machine, composed of integrated land and air forces, will deal with the problem in no uncertain manner.

7. And having crossed the Rhine, we will crack about in the plains of Northern Germany, chasing the enemy from pillar to post. The swifter and the more energetic our action, the sooner the war will be over, and that is what we all desire; to get on with the job and finish off the German war as soon as possible.
8. Over the Rhine, then, let us go. And good hunting to you all on the other side.
9. May 'The Lord mighty in battle' give us the victory in this our latest undertaking, as He has done in all our battles since we landed in Normandy on D-Day."

The Rhine, which in 21st Army Group's sector is about 400 yards wide and has a current of about six feet per second, was the "great obstacle" of which Montgomery spoke. But the means given him to cross it were also great.

Under his command he had two armies, eight corps, and 27 divisions (17 infantry, eight armoured, and two airborne; or, in national terms, 13 American, 12 British, and two Canadian). To these should be added the equivalent of three divisions represented by five armoured brigades, a British commando brigade, and the Canadian 9th Infantry Brigade.

The British 2nd Army's attack, supplemented by the Canadian II Corps, was prepared for and supported by 1,300 pieces of artillery, with 600 guns fulfilling the same function for XVI Corps, which was to open the right bank of the Rhine for the American 9th Army. Such concentration of firepower necessitated the transport and dumping of 60,000 tons of ammunition. Massive area bombing by the Allied air forces extended the artillery action to the Germans' rear areas, thus isolating the battlefield. Between March 20 and 22, R.A.F. Bomber Command and the U.S. 8th and 9th Air Forces made 16,000 sorties over the area in question and dropped 49,500 tons of bombs (including 22,000-lb "Grand

Slams").

To build bridges across the Rhine, 30,000 tons of engineering equipment and 59,000 engineers had to be transported to the area. But before the construction required by Operation "Plunder" could be used, divisions in the first line of attack had to be conveyed from one bank to the other by other means. This task was carried out by a detachment of the Royal Navy, which left Antwerp to reach its departure point by a series of Belgian, Dutch, and German canals. With Vice-Admiral Sir Harold M. Burrough in overall command, it comprised 45 landing craft (L.C.M.), plus a formation of the 12-ton amphibious tanks known by the British as Buffaloes and as Alligators by the Americans. Preparations on this scale were obviously observable by the enemy, but the final deployment of the Allied forces was concealed by the smokescreen which hid the left bank of the Rhine over a distance of 75 miles between dawn on March 21 and 1700 hours on March 23.

As is apparent, Montgomery had once more showed his immense capacity for organisation. In the course of the battle which followed, he would confirm his reputation as an exceptional tactician, by winning back for himself the advantage of surprise which he had lost as a result of such tremendous concentration of forces. And, it should be noted, there are few men who, like him, combine such attention to detail in preparation with such vigour of execution.

On the right bank of the Rhine, the 1st Parachute Army was deployed with its right slightly upstream of Emmerich and its left in the region of Duisburg. It was thus defending a front of 45 miles with seven divisions, an adequate concentration for defence, bearing in mind the natural obstacle of the broad river, had the divisions been at full complement. During the relative lull following March 11, they had dug themselves in well and the rapid construction of their defensive positions was entirely satisfactory to Kesselring. General Schlemm had played a considerable rôle here; Major Milton Shulman, of the Canadian 1st Army, had the opportunity of interrogating him later, and writes:

"His record, coupled with an orderly mind and a keen grasp of tactical problems, placed him amongst the more able generals still available in the Wehrmacht."

However, faced by Montgomery's eight divisions and five armoured brigades, Schlemm's only mobile reserves were the 116th Panzer and 15th *Panzergrenadier* Divisions, of XLVII Panzer Corps, which he had put in reserve behind his centre. At a higher command level, in Army Group "H", Colonel-General Blaskowitz was similarly short of men, and the meagre reserves found by Kesselring were spent in containing the twin thrust of the American 1st Army bursting out of the Remagen bridgehead, and the 3rd Army exploiting at record speed the bridgeheads it had won at Hanau and Aschaffenburg on the Main.

O.K.W. and O.B. West confidently expected an airborne landing. Accordingly, an entire anti-aircraft corps was put at the disposal of Blaskowitz, who deployed batteries all over the area between Munster and the right bank of the Rhine. But apparently to little effect:

▵ *The disillusionment of defeat on the face of a 16-year old captured by the Americans.*
▹ *U.S. troops move off towards the front after crossing the Rhine.*

as on previous occasions the German soldier had to put up with implacable and practically unchallenged machine gun and cannon fire and bombing from Allied aircraft without seeing any fighters of his own in the sky.

The battle begins

At 1700 hours on March 23, the smoke-screen vanished and the entire artillery of the British 2nd Army and the American 9th Army opened fire on the enemy positions, maintaining their barrage of shells of all calibres until 0945 hours the following morning. This was, however, interspersed with pauses at times varying from sector to sector to allow the divisions launching the attack to feel out the enemy strength.

The main action devolved upon the British 2nd Army, in position north of the Lippe. On its left, XXX Corps had during the night got four battalions of the 51st Division (Major-General Thomas Rennie) across the Rhine; on its right, XII Corps had established its 15th Division (Major-General Colin Muir Barber) on the right bank of the river, opposite Xanten, while the 1st Commando Brigade went into action against the 180th Division in the ruins of Wesel. Further south, the American 9th Army, whose task was to cover the flank of the British attack, engaged its XVI Corps, whose 30th and 79th Divisions crossed the Rhine to either side of Rheinberg. According to Montgomery, German resistance was only sporadic, and certainly the two American divisions mentioned above suffered only 31 killed in the enterprise.

The offensive undertaken by the 21st Army Group was no surprise for Blaskowitz, who had even correctly estimated its main point of impact and line of advance. Accordingly–and with a degree of haste for which Kesselring reproached him–he judged it opportune to throw in his armoured reserves. The dawn saw furious counter-attacks which drew the following observation from Sir Brian Horrocks, then in command of XXX Corps:

"Reports were coming in of Germans surrendering in large numbers to the British and American forces on our flanks but there was no sign of any collapse on our front. In fact the 51st Highland Division reported that the enemy was fighting harder than at any time since Normandy. It says a lot for the morale of those German parachute and panzer troops that with chaos, disorganisation and disillusionment all around them they should still be resisting so stubbornly."

In the course of the fighting between XXX Corps and the 15th *Panzergrenadier* Division, which brought into the line the paratroops from the German 6th and 7th Parachute Divisions, Major-General Rennie was killed, evidence enough of the enemy's determination.

Airborne landings

However, at 1000 hours the "event", in the Napoleonic sense of the word, took place. In the German camp, remembering the precedent of Arnhem, the Allies' airborne troops were expected to attack at the time that Montgomery's infantry was attempting to cross the Rhine, and to drop to the rear of the battlefield to effect a vertical encirclement of the 1st Parachute Army. But their attack came three hours after it had been anticipated, and the drop took place in the region of Hamminkeln, barely five miles from the right bank of the river. Under the command of Lieutenant-General Matthew B. Ridgway, XVIII Airborne Corps comprised the British 6th Airborne (Major-General E. Bols) and the American 17th Airborne (Major-General William E. Miley) Divisions, their transport being undertaken by 1,572 planes and 1,326 gliders, under close escort from 889 fighters. The 6th Airborne Division took off from 11 airfields in the south-east of England, the American 17th from 17 that had just been built in the area bounded by Rheims, Orléans, Evreux, and Amiens. The effect of surprise was so great and the German *flak* so well neutralised by Allied artillery pounding from the left bank that losses on landing amounted to no more than 46 transport planes and three per cent of the glider force employed in this operation, known as "Varsity".

The British and Americans fell on the enemy battery positions and reduced a good many of them to silence, then thrust on across the Diersforterwald to meet XII Corps, whose advance was strongly supported by 580 heavy guns of the 2nd Army, responding to calls for fire cover with most admirable speed and precision.

At the end of the day, XVIII Airborne Corps made contact with the British XII Corps. Furthermore, thanks to units flown in by glider, XVIII Airborne Corps had taken intact a number of bridges over the IJssel which, flowing as it does parallel to the Rhine between Wesel and Emmerich, could have constituted an obstacle to the rapid exploitation of the day's successes. Moreover, the 84th Division was taken in rear and as good as annihilated, with the loss of most of the 3,789 prisoners counted by General Ridgway's Intelligence services.

Large bridgehead

As night fell, in the zone between Dinslaken and Rees, where resistance from German parachute troops had lost none of its spirit, the 21st Army Group had taken a bridgehead 30 miles wide on the right bank of the Rhine, running, in the British XII Corps' (Lieutenant-General Sir Neil Methuen Ritchie) sector to a depth of nearly eight miles; the Allied bridge builders were free to get to work without any threat of retaliation on the part of enemy artillery. Montgomery could feel all the more satisfaction with the way things had gone on March 24 as he had committed only four of his eight corps.

Eisenhower's excellent plan

From an observation post situated a mile or so south of Xanten, which commanded a good view over the vast Westphalian plain, Churchill, together with Brooke and Eisenhower, saw the British and American XVIII Airborne Corps' transport planes cross overhead and return, but missed the drop itself because of the mist. As the success of the operation became apparent, General Eisenhower reports that Field-Marshal Brooke turned to him and said:

"Thank God, Ike, you stuck by your plan. You were completely right, and I am sorry if my fear of dispersed effort added to your burdens. The German is now licked. It is merely a question of when he chooses to quit. Thank God, you stuck by your guns."

△ △ ◁ *American infantry embark on an L.C.V.(P.) to cross the Rhine.*
△ ◁ *Men of the U.S. 7th Army prepare to cross south of Worms in outboard engine-powered "Duck" craft.*
◁ *Chaffee light tanks of the U.S. 9th Army and their transport.*
△ *Troops of the 7th Army embark during the morning of March 26.*
▷ *A pensive moment just before the landings for infantry of the 7th Army.*

The American M22 Locust air-transportable light tank

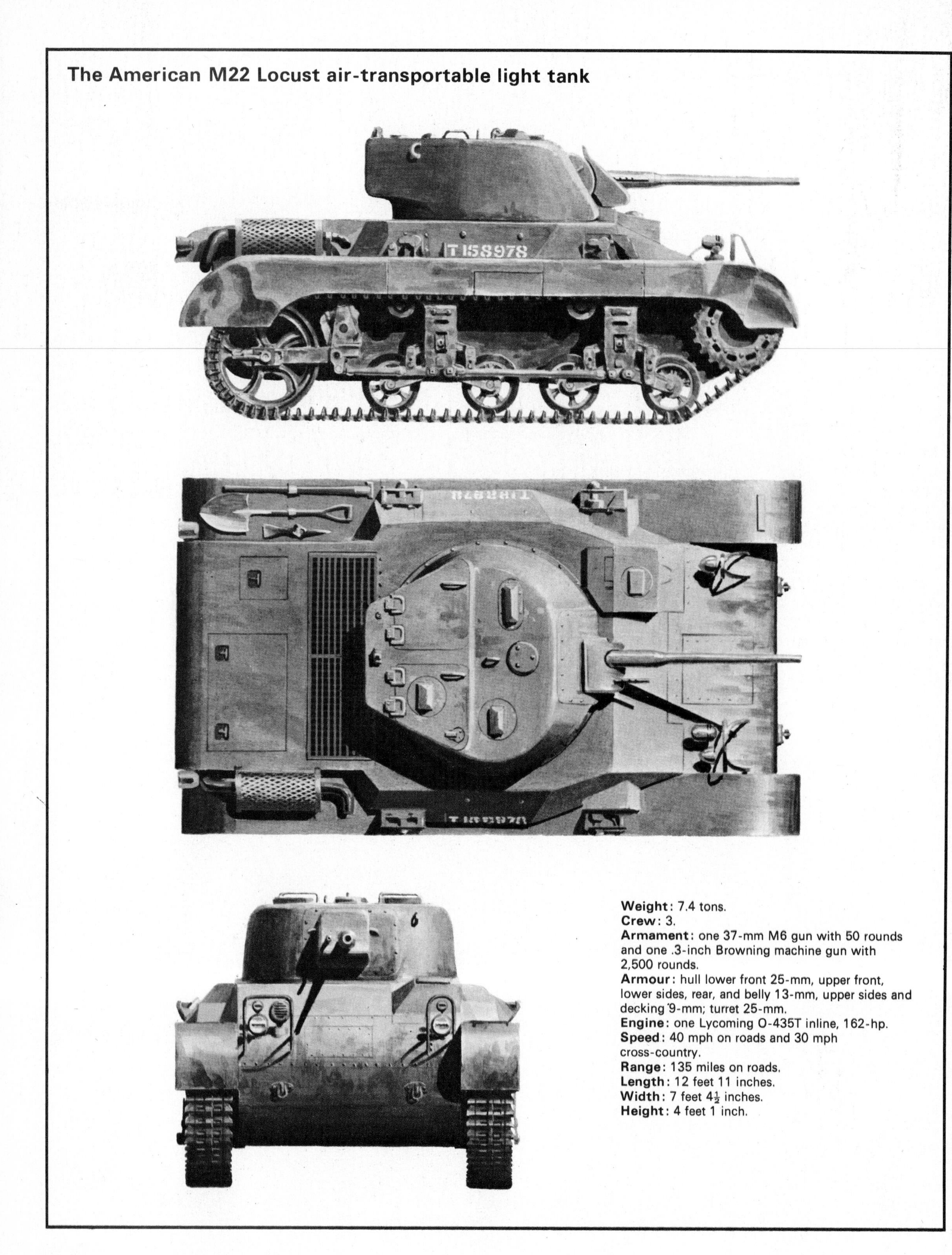

Weight: 7.4 tons.
Crew: 3.
Armament: one 37-mm M6 gun with 50 rounds and one .3-inch Browning machine gun with 2,500 rounds.
Armour: hull lower front 25-mm, upper front, lower sides, rear, and belly 13-mm, upper sides and decking 9-mm; turret 25-mm.
Engine: one Lycoming O-435T inline, 162-hp.
Speed: 40 mph on roads and 30 mph cross-country.
Range: 135 miles on roads.
Length: 12 feet 11 inches.
Width: 7 feet 4½ inches.
Height: 4 feet 1 inch.

Coming across this passage in *Crusade in Europe,* Lord Alanbrooke refers to an entry in his diary made at the close of that same March 24, claiming that Eisenhower's remarks resulted from a misunderstanding, and that he had not in fact "seen the light" that day near Xanten. He wrote in 1949:

"To the best of my memory I congratulated him heartily on his success and said that, as matters had turned out, his policy was now the correct one; that, with the German in his defeated condition, no dangers now existed in a dispersal of effort."

Thus Brooke corrects the remark attributed to him (on this occasion) by Eisenhower. Obviously there is a difference between the two versions. Nevertheless, it does not necessarily follow that Eisenhower was mistaken in defending his strategic plans, unless it can be shown that the German armies would have fallen into the state of ruin and confusion noted by Brooke that March 25 evening had not Operations "Lumberjack" and "Undertone" taken place.

Kesselring settles that question with greater authority than we can possibly lay claim to when he writes:

"Just as Remagen became the tomb of Army Group 'B', the Oppenheim bridgehead seemed destined to become that of Army Group 'G'. There too, the initial pocket became a deep chasm, and devoured all the strength of the other parts of the front, that somehow or other had been rendered mobile, as well as all the units brought up from the rear to fill the gaps."

Collapse of the German 15th Army

On March 25 and 28, two further events of comparable scale and importance took place on the 12th Army Group's front: firstly, the collapse of the German 15th Army, whose task it was to contain the enemy within the Remagen bridgehead; and secondly, adding its effect to the clean breakthrough by the American 1st Army, the crossing of the Main at the Aschaffenburg and Hanau bridges by the American 3rd Army. This manoeuvre followed from a carefully prepared plan of General Bradley's after the launching of Operation "Lumberjack", which was given its final touches following the surprise assault on Remagen. He describes it as follows in *A Soldier's Story:*

"Now that Hodges had established the Remagen bridgehead to the south of Bonn, he was to trace that original pattern. First he would speed his tanks down the autobahn where it ran through Limburg on the road to Frankfurt. At Limburg he was to turn east up the Lahn Valley to Giessen. There he would join Patton's pincer coming up from the Main.

"The First and Third Armies would then advance abreast of one another in a parallel column with Hodges on the inside, Patton on his flank, up the broad Wetteran corridor toward a union with Simpson. Then while Hodges and Simpson locked themselves around the Ruhr preparatory to cleaning it out, Patton would face his Army to the east and be prepared to advance toward the oncoming Russians."

So it was, but according to Kesselring, the execution of Bradley's plan was considerably eased by Model's preconceived ideas of the enemy's intentions. The commander of Army Group "B" was obsessed with his right flank, fearing an attack down the eastern bank of the Rhine aimed at an assault on the Ruhr industrial complex from the south; and he was deaf to all telephone calls from his superior, remonstrating with him for leaving his centre thinly protected.

On March 25, the American 1st Army

△ *Supplies for the 9th Army arrive by D.U.K.W. and jeep on the east bank of the Rhine.*

▵ *Sherman tanks roll into the ruins of Munster on April 3.*

proved Kesselring's case by smashing LXXIV Corps in the region of Breitscheid. Hodges immediately unleashed his 3rd, 7th, and 9th Armoured Divisions, which reached Giessen and Marburg on the 28th, 53 and 66 miles respectively from the Rhine at Neuwied. On the same day, in the 3rd Army, VIII Corps completed the mopping up of Frankfurt and made contact with Hodges's right in the region of Wiesbaden, thus trapping the enemy elements left on the right bank of the Rhine between the Lahn and the Main. But most strikingly, Patton's 4th, 6th, and 11th Armoured Divisions, in formation ahead of XII and XX Corps, had moved from the Main valley into that of the Fulda, making in the direction of Kassel. Thus Hodges, whose task was to reach the eastern outlets of the Ruhr basin, found himself provided with cover, just as Bradley intended, against a counter-attack striking from the Harz mountains.

The Ruhr pocket

On the day after the surprise breakthrough at Oppenheim, Kesselring, according to his own account, had wondered "whether it was not best to accept the army groups' proposals and

withdraw the entire front from the Rhine. I finally refrained from doing so, because the only result would have been to retreat in disorder. Our troops were heavily laden, barely mobile, in large part battle-weary, and encumbered by units in the rear which were still in a state of disorder. The enemy had all-round superiority, especially in mobility and in the air. If nothing occurred to check or slow his advance, our retreating columns would be overtaken and smashed. This type of combat would have become an end in itself–no longer a means employed to an end–the end being to gain time. Every day on the Rhine, on the contrary, was a day gained, signifying a strengthening of the front, even if it were only to enable points in the rear to be mopped up or stray troops to be rounded up."

Quite clearly, at the point reached in the German camp on March 28, Kesselring's conclusions were still more justified.

This was all the more true as the sappers of the 21st Army Group had by March 26 opened seven 40-ton bridges to traffic, and the American 9th Army and British 2nd Army came down both banks of the Lippe to overwhelm the 1st Parachute Army. Two days later, on the left bank of this river, Lieutenant-General Simpson had his 8th Armoured Division (Major-General J. M. Devine) in the region of Haltern, more than 25 miles east of the Rhine. At the same time, Sir Miles Dempsey pushed the Guards Armoured Division (Major-General Allan Adair) down the Münster road, while his XXX and Canadian II Corps, on a line linking Borken – Bocholt – Isselburg – Emmerich, reached the Dutch frontier. The 1st Parachute Army was helplessly cut off, and its LXIII Corps and XLVII Panzer Corps (five divisions) were thrown back onto Army Group "B". And Montgomery poured his armoured units resolutely into the breach.

On April 2, 1945, as the day closed, the inevitable happened. The American 3rd Armoured Division, driving ahead of VII Corps (1st Army), met up at Lippstatt with the 8th Armoured Division coming from Haltern. In the course of this fighting, Major-General Rose, commanding the 3rd Armoured Division in its finest foray, was killed. Now Army Group "B" was encircled, with the exception of LXVII Corps, which had been attached to Army Group "B" following the breakthrough at Breitscheid.

Including the ruins of the 1st Parachute Army mentioned above, there were the 5th *Panzerarmee* and the 15th Army, of seven corps or 19 divisions (three of them Panzer, and the 3rd *Panzergrenadier* Division) caught in a trap that Hitler was quick to qualify as "the fortified region of the Ruhr". To reduce it, General Bradley formed a new 15th Army, under the command of Lieutenant-General Leonard T. Gerow, with a strength of five corps, including the newly-formed XXII and XXIII Corps, in all 18 divisions taken from the 1st and 9th Armies.

The encirclement of the Ruhr meant not only the rapid destruction of Army Group "B", but more importantly, the end of all organised resistance on the

▵ *Ulm Cathedral, surprisingly undamaged amidst the debris of the rest of the city.*

part of the Wehrmacht between Würzburg on the Main and Minden on the Weser. Between the inside of the wings of Army Groups "G" and "H", a breach of more than 180 miles was opened. It was too late for the unfortunate Kesselring to cherish the notion of repositioning his armies on a line along the courses of the Weser, Werra, Main, Altmuhl, and Lech, as favoured by 18th Century strategists.

Eisenhower gives up the idea of Berlin . . .

To stop this breach, O.K.W. still had, in the Harz mountains, the 11th Army, comprising five divisions under the command of General Wenck, and a 12th Army being formed on the right bank of the Elbe. But clearly the way to Berlin lay open to the 12th Army Group and on April 4 S.H.A.E.F. reinforced it with the American 9th Army, to the great satisfaction of General Simpson, its commander, and even more so of General Bradley, who saw the forces under his command now rise to four armies (11 corps of 48 divisions, 14 of them armoured, with some 3,600 tanks). But Eisenhower had no intention of giving Bradley the German capital as an objective. The question had already been considered by him among other options open to him after the encirclement of the Ruhr, and he had decided against going for Berlin for strategic and logistic reasons–in particular the lengthening of his lines of communication that this would entail, and the obstacle of the Elbe, something short of 200 miles from the Rhine and 125 from Berlin.

As a result of this decision, Eisenhower set himself the following objectives:

1. to make contact without delay with the Soviet forces moving west, and thus make it impossible for the enemy to try to regroup;
2. to hurl the 21st Army Group to the north-east, its right wing keeping its objective steadily fixed on Lübeck, to cut off the Wehrmacht forces occupying Norway and Denmark; and
3. for the 12th and 6th Army Groups, Eisenhower writes:

"Equally important was the desirability of penetrating and destroying the so-called 'National Redoubt'. For many weeks we had been receiving reports that the Nazi intention, in extremity, was to withdraw the cream of the S.S., Gestapo, and other organisations fanatically devoted to Hitler, into the mountains of southern Bavaria, western Austria, and northern Italy. There they expected to block the tortuous mountain passes and to hold out indefinitely against the Allies. Such a stronghold could always be reduced by eventual starvation if in no other way. But if the German was permitted to establish the redoubt he might possibly force us to engage in a long-drawn-out guerrilla type of warfare, or a costly siege. Thus he could keep alive his desperate hope that through disagreement among the Allies he might yet be able to secure terms more favourable than those of unconditional surrender. The evidence was clear that the Nazi intended to make the attempt and I decided to give him no opportunity to carry it out."

So, with the Elbe reached in the vicinity of Magdeburg, it was understood that Bradley would make his main line of advance along a line Erfurt–Leipzig–Dresden, with a secondary thrust on Regensburg and Linz. Contact would be made with the Russians in Saxony, and at the same time a march would be stolen on Army Group "G" in its task of occupying the redoubt. However logical this line of argument was from a strategic point of view, it rested on a hypothesis which was shown to be false after Germany's capitulation: the "national redoubt" concept was no more than a figment of the imagination of those who fed it to S.H.A.E.F.'s Intelligence services.

Stalin approves warmly . . .

In any event, on March 24, in accordance with a decision taken at the Yalta Conference, Eisenhower communicated his plan, summarised above, to Stalin who approved it most warmly. In the terms of a telegram cited in Churchill's memoirs but absent from *Crusade in Europe*, Stalin assured Eisenhower that his plan "entirely coincides with the plan of the Soviet High Command . . . Berlin has lost its former strategic importance. The Soviet High Command therefore plans to allot secondary forces in the direction of Berlin." Knowing as we do that at the very moment these lines were dictated,

▽ *A huge column of German prisoners wends its way back towards the American rear along one of the* Autobahns *constructed by the Nazis to move troops and equipment swiftly–but with a different aim in mind.*

Stalin was concentrating five tank armies and 25,000 guns (expending 25,600 tons of shell) on an allegedly secondary objective, one sees what was in the wind.

. . . but Churchill objects violently

The plan elaborated by S.H.A.E.F. found its strongest opponent in Churchill. Embodying as he did the ancient traditions which had inspired British diplomacy since the reign of Henry VIII, he held as a maxim that "as a war waged by a coalition draws to its end political aspects have a mounting importance."

So it seemed obvious to him that since the military collapse of the Third Reich was a matter of only a few weeks, the time had come for the two great Anglo-Saxon powers quietly to dismiss purely strategic considerations and consider political issues while there was still time. And in this field he was forced to admit that Stalin and Molotov viewed the Yalta agreement about Poland as being worth no more than the paper it was written on, and were set in their determination to allow no régime in Warsaw that was not subservient to Moscow.

Likewise, on March 2, Vishinsky, Soviet Deputy Minister of Foreign Affairs, in the course of a scene of abominable violence, had imposed a government chosen by the Kremlin on King Michael of Rumania. The ten per cent minority voice that Churchill had reserved in that country had fallen to all but nothing, and things were worse still in Bulgaria.

Hence Churchill thought that future operations conducted by S.H.A.E.F. should take account of political as well as military considerations, and these he enumerated and summarised as follows:

"*First,* that Soviet Russia had become a mortal danger to the free world.

▽ *American armour rumbles through the streets of Mönchengladbach in the Ruhr industrial area.*

Lt.-Gen. Sir Miles Dempsey was born in 1896 and first came to prominence at the head of XIII Corps in the Sicilian and Italian campaigns. Before the Normandy landings he was promoted to command the 2nd Army, which he then led up to the end of the war, winning a considerable reputation for committing his men to major actions only when he was convinced that success was almost certain.

Lt.-Gen. Henry Crerar was born in 1888 and served with the Canadian artillery in World War I. From 1935 to 1938 he was Director of Military Operations and Intelligence. He was Chief-of-Staff of the Canadian Army in 1940. He commanded the Canadian I Corps and later the 1st Army in Europe.

Secondly, that a new front must be immediately created against her onward sweep.
Thirdly, that this front in Europe should be as far east as possible.
Fourthly, that Berlin was the prime and true objective of the Anglo-American armies.
Fifthly, that the liberation of Czechoslovakia and the entry into Prague of American troops was of high consequence.
Sixthly, that Vienna, and indeed Austria, must be regulated by the Western Powers, at least upon an equality with the Russian Soviets.
Seventhly, that Marshal Tito's aggressive pretensions against Italy must be curbed.
Finally, and above all, that a settlement must be reached on all major issues between the West and the East *before the armies of democracy melted,* or the Western Allies yielded any part of the German territories they had conquered, or, as it could soon be written, liberated from totalitarian tyranny."

Eisenhower's plan therefore displeased him all the more because in communicating his intentions to Stalin, the Supreme Allied Commander appeared to have exceeded the commonly accepted limits of competence of a military chief; a somewhat dubious argument since Stalin had concentrated in himself the functions of head of government and generalissimo of the Soviet armed forces, in which capacity the communication had been addressed to him. With the approval of the British Chief-of-Staffs Committee and of Montgomery, the Prime Minister endeavoured to persuade Eisenhower to go back on his decision, and on April 1 an appeal was made to President Roosevelt, Field-Marshal Brooke making a similar appeal to General Marshall.

Eisenhower refuses to countermand his orders

But Eisenhower refused to give in. On March 31, when giving his instructions to Montgomery, he pointedly wrote:

"You will note that in none of this do I mention Berlin. That place has become, so far as I am concerned, nothing but a geographical location, and I have never been interested in these. My purpose is to destroy the enemy's forces and powers to resist."

On the next day Eisenhower received a telegram from the American Joint Chiefs-of-Staff, telling him that despite the objections of the British chiefs, they supported him entirely, and that, in particular, the communication of his future plans to Stalin seemed to them "to be a necessity dictated by operations". Marshall concluded with the following point to his allies:

"To deliberately turn away from the exploitation of the enemy's weakness does not appear sound. The single objective should be quick and complete victory. While recognising there are factors not of direct concern to S.C.A.E.F., the U.S. chiefs consider his strategic concept is sound and should receive full support. He should continue to communicate freely with the Commander-in-Chief of the Soviet Army."

In his memoirs, Montgomery, when dealing with this difference of opinion, quotes from a letter on the subject written to him by Eisenhower on September 15 of the previous year:

"*Clearly, Berlin is the main prize.* There is no doubt whatsoever, in my mind, that we should concentrate all our energies and resources on a rapid thrust to Berlin."

"But now he did not agree," adds Montgomery.

Nonetheless, the situation had to some extent changed between September 15,

1944, and the close of March 1945. In particular, the Russians had moved forward from the Vistula to the Oder, and S.H.A.E.F. believed that Hitler and his principal collaborators were preparing to abandon Berlin and make for the alleged "national redoubt". Hence the Reich capital would seem to have lost considerably in value as an objective.

One might be justified in concluding from this that in disregarding Berlin as the proper objective, Eisenhower, far from showing proof of versatility, was simply applying with some obtuseness the teaching he had absorbed at West Point: namely that the first and foremost objective of any strategy worthy of the name consists in destroying the forces of the enemy, and that a great general should never subordinate this to geographical objectives, however commanding they appear. Marshall, too, had been trained in the same principles. Added to this, both men were the less inclined to heed the advice of Brooke and Montgomery, whose criticism of the "broad front" and the dual attack on the Rhine had been invalidated by the course of recent events.

An order from Roosevelt, in his capacity as head of the American armed forces, would most certainly have led them to review their point of view purely and simply as military leaders. But no such order came. Here Roosevelt stuck to his principle of not intervening in matters of strategy; but even had he desired to do so, his health had now deteriorated to such an extent that he was no longer capable of making such decisions. According to Churchill, the Western powers found themselves in "the deadly hiatus which existed between the fading of President Roosevelt's strength and the growth of President Truman's grip of the vast world problem. In this melancholy void one President could not act and the other could not know. Neither the military chiefs nor the State Department received the guidance they required. The former confined themselves to their professional sphere; the latter did not comprehend the issues involved."

The facts could scarcely be better put. But it should not go unsaid that in his appeal to Roosevelt, Churchill was understandably less trenchant than later in his memoirs, with the world for his audience; he based his case for the occupation of Berlin on the following hypothesis:

"The Russian armies will no doubt overrun all Austria and enter Vienna. If they also take Berlin will not their impression that they have been the overwhelming contributor to our common victory be unduly imprinted in their minds, and may this not lead them into a mood which will raise grave and formidable difficulties in the future?"

△ ◁ *M26 Pershing tanks of the American 9th Army's 2nd Armoured Division pass the wrecked town hall of Magdeburg.*
△ *An American M36 90-mm Motor Gun Carriage crosses the Rhine to reinforce the Allied troops clawing their way into Germany.*

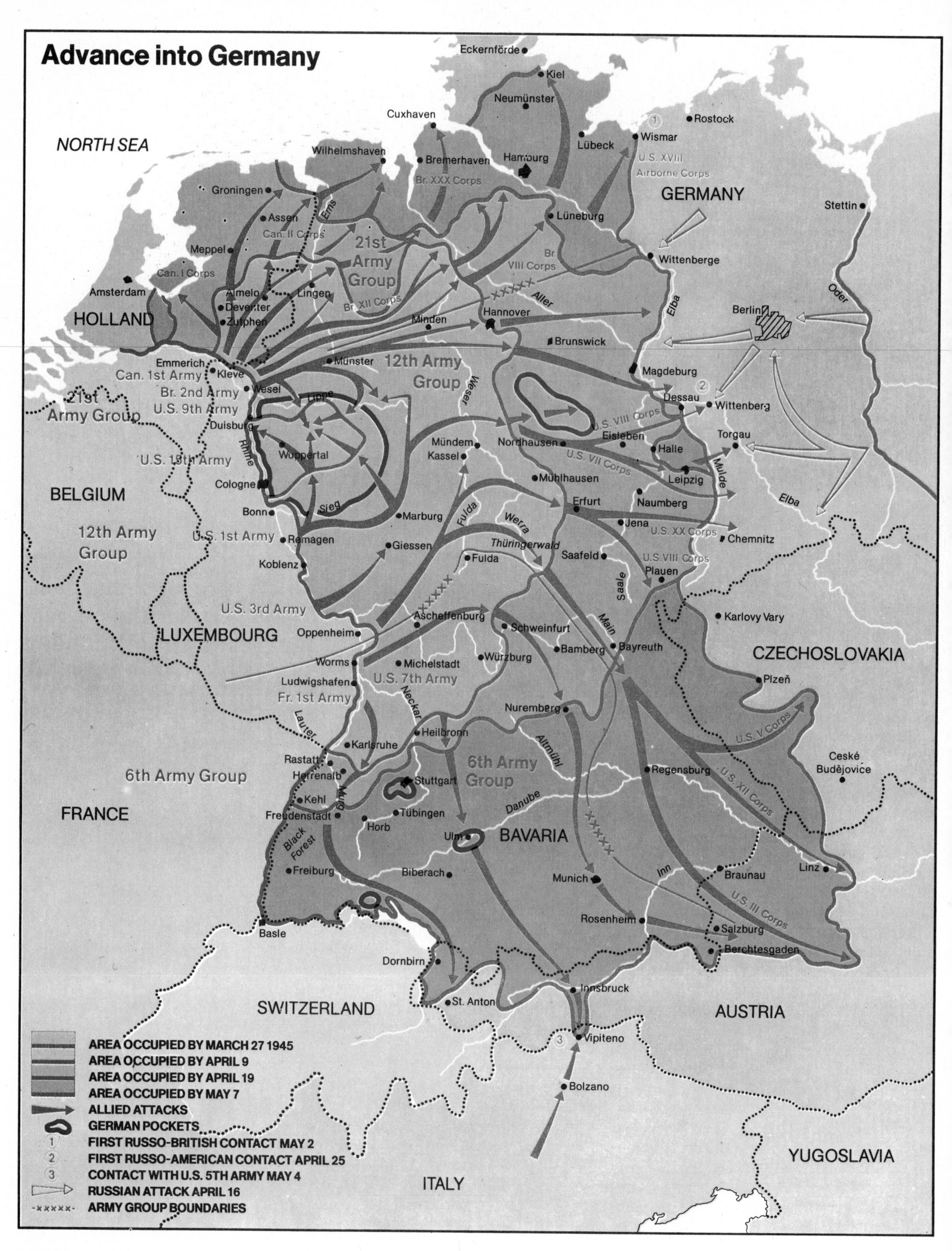
Advance into Germany
NORTH SEA
Eckernförde
Kiel
Neumünster
Cuxhaven
Rostock
Wismar
Lübeck
Wilhelmshaven
Bremerhaven
Hamburg
U.S. XVIII Airborne Corps
Br. XXX Corps
Groningen
GERMANY
Stettin
Assen
Lüneburg
Can. II Corps
Ems
21st Army Group
Meppel
Wittenberge
Br. VIII Corps
Can. I Corps
Almelo
Lingen
Aller
Amsterdam
Deventer
Br. XII Corps
Oder
Zutphen
Hannover
Elba
Berlin
HOLLAND
Minden
Brunswick
Emmerich
Münster
12th Army Group
Magdeburg
Can. 1st Army
Kleve
Br. 2nd Army
Wesel
Weser
21st Army Group
U.S. 9th Army
Lippe
Dessau
Wittenberg
Duisburg
U.S. VIII Corps
Rhine
Mündem
Nordhausen
Eisleben
Torgau
U.S. 15th Army
Wuppertal
Kassel
Halle
U.S. VII Corps
Mulde
Leipzig
Cologne
Mühlhausen
BELGIUM
Erfurt
Naumberg
Sieg
Bonn
Marburg
Fulda
Werra
Elba
12th Army Group
Jena
U.S. 1st Army
Remagen
U.S. XX Corps
Chemnitz
Giessen
Thüringerwald
Koblenz
Fulda
Saafeld
U.S. VIII Corps
Plauen
Saale
U.S. 3rd Army
Karlovy Vary
Ascheffenburg
Schweinfurt
Main
LUXEMBOURG
Oppenheim
Bamberg
Bayreuth
CZECHOSLOVAKIA
Worms
Michelstadt
Würzburg
U.S. 7th Army
Ludwigshafen
Plzeň
Fr. 1st Army
Neckar
Lauter
Nuremberg
U.S. V Corps
Heilbronn
Altmühl
Karlsruhe
Rastatt
6th Army Group
České Budějovice
6th Army Group
Regensburg
Herrenalb
Stuttgart
U.S. XII Corps
Kehl
Murg
Danube
FRANCE
Freudenstadt
Tübingen
Horb
Ulm
BAVARIA
Black Forest
Linz
Freiburg
Biberach
Munich
Inn
Braunau
U.S. III Corps
Rosenheim
Salzburg
Basle
Berchtesgaden
Dornbirn
Innsbruck
SWITZERLAND
St. Anton
AUSTRIA
Vipiteno
Bolzano
YUGOSLAVIA
ITALY
AREA OCCUPIED BY MARCH 27 1945
AREA OCCUPIED BY APRIL 9
AREA OCCUPIED BY APRIL 19
AREA OCCUPIED BY MAY 7
ALLIED ATTACKS
GERMAN POCKETS
FIRST RUSSO-BRITISH CONTACT MAY 2
FIRST RUSSO-AMERICAN CONTACT APRIL 25
CONTACT WITH U.S. 5TH ARMY MAY 4
RUSSIAN ATTACK APRIL 16
ARMY GROUP BOUNDARIES

CHAPTER 148

The End in Italy

by Lt.-Col. Alan Shepperd

▵ *Sherman tank of the U.S. 1st Armoured Division moves up towards Lucca before the campaign to break the Gothic Line.*

Originally known as the Apennine Position, the Gothic Line ran across the mountains, coast to coast, for 200 miles, from near La Spezia on the Gulf of Genoa to Pesaro on the Adriatic. It was longer than the line through Cassino, and the mountain barrier reached across the peninsula to within a short distance of Route 16, which followed the coast-line through the narrow plain to Rimini. Orders for the line to be reconnoitred and fortified had in fact been given by Jodl almost a month before the evacuation of Sicily, but more recently the work had been interrupted by the pressing demands for *matériel* and labour for building the defences of the Gustav and Hitler Lines.

At the time of the capture of Rome, Alexander estimated that Kesselring would have only the equivalent of ten divisions to man the Apennine positions, but Hitler's immediate reaction to the threat of an Allied advance into northern Italy had completely changed the situation. Kesselring was now able to gain much-needed time for the Organisation Todt to complete most of the defences that had been so carefully planned.

At the very height of the fighting in Normandy, Hitler dispatched no less than seven divisions, withdrawn from Denmark, Holland, Hungary, and even the Russian front, to reinforce Army Group "C" in Italy. Finally O.K.W. sent a battalion of Tiger tanks from

▽ *German reinforcements en route to the Italian front. The two vehicles in the foreground are ex-Austrian Army "Mulus" wheeled/tracked carriers, and the conventional vehicles appear to be civilian vehicles taken over by the military.*

France and the whole of three divisions, forming in Germany, to fill up the ranks of the infantry divisions that had been virtually annihilated in the Liri valley.

Although Alexander had been warned as early as May 22, 1944, that he must be prepared to provide seven divisions for a landing in the south of France, it was not until July 5, when the battle for Arezzo was in the balance and the Polish II Corps was still short of Ancona, that he was told that his pleas to be allowed to keep his force intact, for a thrust into northern Italy and beyond, had finally been turned down.

The task that Alexander was now given was:

1. to cross the Apennines to the line of the River Po; and
2. to cross the river and seize the line Venice – Padua – Verona – Brescia.

After this he would receive further instructions.

In spite of the loss of so many divisions, including the French Expeditionary Corps with all its mountain troops, the Allied offensive must continue. Once again Kesselring would have superiority in numbers on the ground and strongly fortified positions on which to make his stand. The summer days were running out and the chance of any large scale penetration into the Po valley before winter set in now appeared most unlikely. But in Normandy the Battle of Caen was about to start–it was imperative that the pressure by the Allies in Italy should be maintained, even increased.

So long as there had been hopes of a rapid advance, the bridges over the Po had been spared by the Allied bombers. On July 12 the Tactical Air Force went to work and in three days cut all 23 of the rail and road bridges over the river. The battle for the Gothic Line had begun.

Superb defences

In the mountains the German engineers had already constructed a series of strong-points astride the routes leading to the Po valley at Borgo a Mozzano, Porretta, the Vernio pass north of Prato, and the Futa and Il Giogo passes north of Florence. From here the line ran south-east, again with every route blocked, from Casaglia to below Bagno and the Mandrioli pass, before turning eastwards to drop down to the valley of the Foglia and Pesaro on the Adriatic. Here, in the narrow coastal plain, was Route 16, the only road that the Allies could take which did not entail climb across the great mountain barrier. This corridor, however, between the foot-hills and the sea, was cut across by numerous rivers; and the succession of ridges, which similarly were at right angles to the line of advance, was admirably suited for defence. Moreover, the rivers were liable to sudden flooding and rain quickly turned the heavy soil into a sea

Δ *German infantry move down through the Dolomites from Austria towards the front.*

of mud. The fortifications in this sector had been skilfully prepared, with anti-tank ditches, extensive minefields, and the usual deep bunkers. In June and July, while Kesselring's rearguards were slowly falling back through Lombardy, Todt engineers, with thousands of conscripted Italian labourers, were frantically engaged in constructing a ten mile deep belt of obstacles along the whole line, and in the mountains a series of positions to link up with the main strongholds, so as to form a continuous front. A report on the defences that had been completed when the battle started listed 2,376 machine gun nests, 479 anti-tank gun, mortar, and assault gun positions, 120,000 yards of wire entanglement, and many miles of anti-tank ditches. Only four out of the 30 7.5-cm Panther gun turrets ordered by O.K.W., however, were in position.

The balance of forces in the opening stages of the forthcoming battle pitted 26 German divisions, including six Panzer and *Panzergrenadier* divisions, and some six Italian divisions, against 20 Allied divisions, which included four armoured divisions. For the Germans the battle would be fought solely on the ground, as the Luftwaffe in Italy was reduced to 170 aircraft, the majority of which were obsolete. The Allies, with some 75 complete squadrons in the Tactical Air Force alone, enjoyed complete air superiority. This advantage, however, would soon be reduced as the weather deteriorated. Meanwhile Kesselring could neither "see over the hill", nor strike out at his enemy's rear communications. In spite of this and a weakness in both artillery and armour, he viewed his task of beating off the coming offensive with growing confidence, especially after an inspection of the defences on his eastern flank.

Throughout the whole campaign the Germans had overestimated the Allied capability to carry out amphibious operations against their rear and Kesselring, sensitive to the preparations for "Dragoon" (as "Anvil" was now named), feared a landing on the Ligurian coast or even in the Gulf of Venice. Consequently he allocated no less than six divisions to coastal defence. A further weakening of his forces resulted from the active resistance, backed by the Communists, of Italian workers in the industrial areas to Mussolini's puppet government. In effect civil war had broken out, and in spite of the arrival of two German-trained Italian divisions the partisans were also beginning to show their true strength in attacks on military depots and lines of communication. Thus there remained only 19 divisions to hold the Gothic Line itself. On the right was the 14th Army, with XIV Panzer Corps allocated to the long mountain stretch from the coast to Empoli, and I Parachute Corps to hold the shorter and more critical central section facing Florence, both with three divisions. In reserve were the inexperienced 20th Luftwaffe Field Divi-

∇ *American motor transport in typical Italian terrain. The problems faced by the attackers in such country were particularly difficult: firstly the logistic difficulties of moving up men and supplies, and then the tactical disadvantage of having to attack uphill.*

sion and the 29th *Panzergrenadier* Division, north of Florence. East of Pontassieve was the 10th Army, with LI Mountain Corps (five divisions) holding the spine of the Apennine range as far as Sansepolcro and LXXVI Panzer Corps in the foothills and coastal plain, again with five divisions, of which two were echeloned back watching the coast. The newly arrived 98th Division was in army reserve around Bologna. This again emphasised Kesselring's preoccupation with the central section of the mountain barrier, which was only 50 miles deep at this point, in spite of his prediction that the attack would be made on the Adriatic flank. Meanwhile the front line remained on the line of the Arno.

Revised plans

Alexander's initial plan was to press an early attack, with both armies side by side, into the mountains on the axis Florence–Bologna. Indeed the cover plan, with fake wireless traffic and soldiers arriving in the Adriatic sector wearing Canadian I Corps flashes, had already started. But this was before Clark's 5th Army was reduced to a single corps and the total strength of both armies to 20 divisions. Moreover there was no chance of any reinforcements other than the U.S. 92nd (Negro) Division in September and a Brazilian division by the end of October. So there could be no diversionary operations and no reserve to maintain the impetus of the advance. In spite of this, General Harding, Alexander's chief-of-staff, recommended the plan should stand. Lieutenant-General Sir Oliver Leese, the 8th Army commander, whose troops would have to bear the brunt of the fighting, felt there was a far better chance of breaking through on the Adriatic sector, where his superiority in tanks and guns could be employed to greater effect.

Furthermore General Clark would have greater freedom to make his own dis-

△ Lieutenant-Colonel J. Sokol, of the Polish 3rd Carpathian Infantry Division, inspects U.S. artillery positions. The division formed part of the Polish II Corps that took Pesaro.

▽ Canadian armour crosses the Sieve, which flows into the Arno at Pontassieve, ten miles east of Florence.

▷ An anti-tank mine clearing platoon of the U.S. 85th Division prepares to clear the approaches to a Bailey bridge being built by the 255th Combat Engineers of the U.S. IV Corps across a gorge on Route 64, south of Bologna.
▽ Vergato, south of Bologna: an M24 Chaffee of the 81st Reconnaissance Squadron of the U.S. 1st Armoured Division rolls confidently into the ruins.
△▷ U.S. infantry south of Bologna.
▽▷ American forces in the Piazza del Campo in Siena.

positions. This plan suited one of Alexander's favourite strategies, the "two-handed punch", in that by striking at both Ravenna and Bologna the enemy's reserves would be split. At a secret meeting on Orvieto airfield on August 4 between the two commanders, with only Harding present, the matter was decided by Alexander in favour of Leese's alternative proposal. As practically the whole of the 8th Army had to be moved across the mountains to the east coast, D-day was put back to August 25. The cover plan was put into reverse, with 5th Army being told to make "ostentatious preparations" for an attack against the centre of the mountain positions. In the greatest secrecy the regrouping of both armies was started immediately.

The transfer to north of Ancona of the bulk of the 8th Army–two complete corps headquarters, some eight divisions, and a mass of corps troops, with over 80,000 vehicles–was achieved in 15 days. This was a remarkable feat as there were only two roads over the mountains, and both had been systematically demolished by the Germans during their retreat. In many places the roads had to be entirely rebuilt and no less than 40 Bailey bridges were constructed by the Royal Engineers before the roads could be reopened. Even so the roads were largely one-way, and the movement tables were further complicated by the need to operate the tank transporters on a continuous shuttle service as a result of the short time available for the concentration of the tank brigades.

Meanwhile the British XIII Corps, of three divisions under Lieutenant-General Sidney Kirkman, joined the U.S. 5th Army, so as to be ready alongside U.S. II Corps to deliver the second blow of "the two-handed punch" towards Bologna. The remaining two U.S. divisions, joined by the 6th South African Armoured Division and a mixed force of American and British anti-aircraft and other support units, hastily trained as infantry, formed Major-General Crittenberger's U.S. IV Corps. This had the task of holding the remainder of the 5th Army front. On the inner flank, acting as a link between the two armies, was X Corps, with the 10th Indian Division, a tank brigade, and several "dismounted" armoured car regiments. Every other available man of the 8th Army was committed to the main assault on the right flank.

Leese's plan was to break into the

▵ *A 2½-ton truck of the Quartermaster's Corps of the U.S. 88th Division surges across a flooded road in the Bologna area, towing another vehicle.*

Gothic Line defences on a narrow front, with the Polish II Corps directed on Pesaro (before going into reserve), and the Canadians making straight for Rimini. The main attack would be through the hills further inland towards Route 9 by Lieutenant-General Sir Charles Keightley's V Corps, with the British 4th, 46th, and 56th, and 1st Armoured Divisions, and 4th Indian Division. The latter was briefed for the pursuit, and would attack alongside the Canadian 5th Armoured Division as soon as the breakthrough was achieved.

The offensive falters

Initially all went well. When the Allied advance started the Germans were engaged in carrying out a series of reliefs in the coastal area, which involved the pulling back of a division from forward positions on the Metauro. Kesselring indeed assumed that the attack on August 25 was no more than a follow-up of this withdrawal. Vietinghoff himself was on leave and only got back late on August 28. The next day the Allied infantry reached the Foglia and Kesselring, who had been taken completely by surprise, at last ordered up reinforcements. But it was too late to stop the penetration of the carefully prepared Gothic Line positions. On August 31 the 46th Division held the formidable bastion of Montegridolfo and the following night Gurkhas of the 4th Indian Division, using only grenades and kukris, captured the strongly fortified town of Tavoleto. In the plain, the Canadians had suffered heavily crossing the river but by dawn on September 3 had a bridgehead across the Conca alongside Route 16. Meanwhile both the 26th Panzer and 98th Divisions had reached the battle area and already suffered heavily.

The way to a breakthrough by V Corps lay in the capture of two hill features, the Coriano and Gemmano Ridges, situated just where the plain begins to widen out. These afforded the Germans excellent observation and fine positions. The task of breaking through was given to the 46th and 56th Divisions. Meanwhile, the British 1st Armoured Division, with some 300 tanks, had already started (on August 31) to move forward in accordance with the original plan. The approach march over narrow and often precipitous tracks, which got progressively worse, proved a nightmare. On one stage "along razor-edged mountain ridges" to reach the Foglia, which was crossed on September 3, drivers of the heavier vehicles had to reverse to get round every corner and some spent 50 hours at the wheel. The tank route proved even more hazardous, and 20 tanks were lost before reaching the assembly area. The driving conditions were extremely exhausting and as the column ground its way forward in low gear many tanks ran out of petrol, while those at the rear of the column were engulfed in dense clouds of choking white dust.

At this critical moment the German 162nd Division and Kesselring's last mobile reserve, the experienced 29th *Panzergrenadier* Division (from Bologna) began to arrive. The renewed attacks

The American M24 Chaffee light tank

Weight: 18 tons.
Crew: 5.
Armament: one 75-mm M6 gun with 48 rounds, and one .5-inch Browning M2 and two .3-inch Browning M1919A4 machine guns with 420 and 4,125 rounds respectively.
Armour: hull front and sides 25-mm, lower sides and rear 19-mm, decking 13-mm, and belly 6.5-mm; turret front and mantlet 38-mm, sides 25-mm, and roof 13-mm.
Engines: two Cadillac Model 44T24 inlines, 110-hp each.
Speed: 30 mph.
Range: 100 miles.
Length: 18 feet.
Width: 9 feet 8 inches.
Height: 8 feet 1½ inches.

▽ 155-mm M1 howitzers of the U.S. 85th Division are towed across the Reno at Pioppi di Salvaro by tracked prime movers.
▷ British infantry rest by a roadside during the closing stages of the Italian campaign. Note the tank destroyers on the road and the weapons carried by the infantry platoon: Lee Enfield rifles, Bren guns, a P.I.A.T. anti-tank weapon, and American M3 sub-machine guns.
▽▷ British infantry bring in two German wounded abandoned by their comrades along the Metauro river.

by V Corps were broken up and held. Into the confused and unresolved struggle the armoured divisions were ordered forward late on September 4. There had been no breakthrough; the fleeting opportunity, if it had ever existed, had passed. The advance of the armoured brigades was met with a storm of shot and shell and an unbroken defence which now included tanks and self-propelled guns. In their advance towards Coriano, the British armoured brigades lost 65 tanks and many more were still struggling to cross the start line as dusk came.

That night rain began to fall and more German reinforcements (from the 356th Division) reached the front. By September 6 the tracks had turned to mud and air strikes could no longer be guaranteed. Alexander now ordered a regrouping for a set-piece attack (on September 12) to clear the two vital ridges. Now was the time for Clark to launch his attack into the mountains.

Since early August Kesselring's front line troops had been kept short of supplies through the interdiction programme of the Allied air forces. With the Brenner pass frequently blocked, north Italy was virtually isolated from the rest of Europe. There was no direct railway traffic across the Po east of Piacenza and south of the river the railway lines down as far as the Arno had been cut in nearly 100 places. But in spite of every difficulty, sufficient supplies were kept moving forward. Each

night, pontoon bridges were built across the Po and then broken up and hidden by day; and ferries were operating at over 50 points on the river.

The Desert Air Force, which had supported the 8th Army so magnificently at a time when almost all the American air effort had been diverted to the "Dragoon" landing, now switched its whole effort to helping Clark's offensive to get under way. Clark's attack came as no surprise to General Joachim Lemelsen, whose 14th Army had already been milked of three divisions to reinforce Colonel-General Heinrich von Vietinghoff's 10th Army. The latter was now seriously short of infantry, and had been ordered to fall back to the prepared defences in

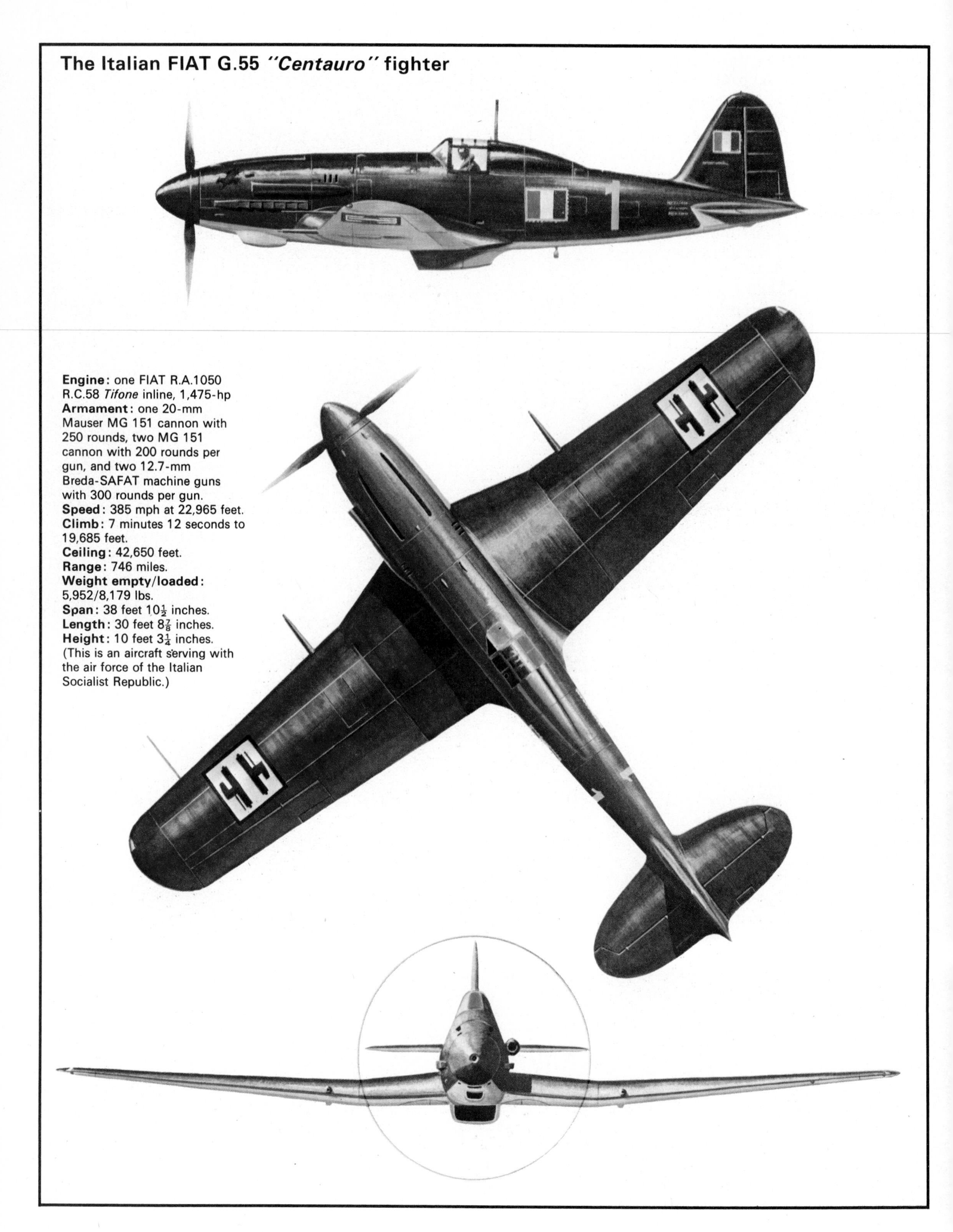

The Italian FIAT G.55 *"Centauro"* fighter

Engine: one FIAT R.A.1050 R.C.58 *Tifone* inline, 1,475-hp
Armament: one 20-mm Mauser MG 151 cannon with 250 rounds, two MG 151 cannon with 200 rounds per gun, and two 12.7-mm Breda-SAFAT machine guns with 300 rounds per gun.
Speed: 385 mph at 22,965 feet.
Climb: 7 minutes 12 seconds to 19,685 feet.
Ceiling: 42,650 feet.
Range: 746 miles.
Weight empty/loaded: 5,952/8,179 lbs.
Span: 38 feet 10½ inches.
Length: 30 feet 8⅞ inches.
Height: 10 feet 3¼ inches.
(This is an aircraft serving with the air force of the Italian Socialist Republic.)

△ *Local intelligence for an American soldier.*

the mountains. Even after the transfer to his command of the 334th Division from the adjacent LI Mountain Corps, Lemelsen had no reserve and with all his force in the line, each division was on at least a ten mile front. From his post on the "touch-line", as it were, in the quiet and inaccessible Ligurian coastal sector, General von Senger und Etterlin correctly forecast the outcome of this impasse. He later wrote:

"The incessant prodding against [the left wing of] our front across the Futa pass was like jabbing a thick cloth with a sharp spear. The cloth would give way like elastic, but under excessive strain it would be penetrated by the spear."

The 5th Army attack was made by two corps and on a narrow front east of the Il Giogo pass, at the junction of the two German armies, and initially fell on two thinly stretched divisions. Holding the Il Giogo pass was the 4th Parachute Division, which had been made up with very young soldiers with barely three months' training. The pass itself was nothing but a way over a ridge only about 2,900 feet high, but overlooked by some of the highest peaks in the whole mountain range.

Clark used Lieutenant-General Geoffrey Keyes's II Corps of four divisions (U.S. 34th, 85th, 88th, and 91st) as his spearhead against the Il Giogo defences. On the tail of the German withdrawal he launched his offensive on September 13. Once again, Kesselring misread the situation. In spite of the efforts of two U.S. divisions, a considerable artillery concentration, and 2,000 sorties by medium and fighter-bombers, the 4th Parachute Division more than held its ground for the first four days. Meanwhile Kirkman's XIII Corps was attacking on the right flank of the Americans along the parallel routes towards Faenza and Forlì. By September 14 the 8th Indian Division was over the watershed and the following day the British 1st Division took Monte Prefetto and, turning to help its neighbours, attacked the German parachute troops on Monte Pratone. As the pressure mounted on the 4th Parachute Division, the leading American infantry began to make ground, and between September 16 and 18 Monti Altuzzo and Monticelli and the nearby strongholds and peaks were captured.

△ *A British officer surveys the final goal of the Italian campaign: the Alps and Austria.*
▷ *Medical corpsmen of the U.S. 10th Mountain Division treat a wounded German prisoner.*

II Corps now held a seven-mile stretch of the Gothic Line defences either side of the Il Giogo pass. At last Kesselring awoke to the danger of a breakthrough to Imola and from either flank rushed in an extra division to hold Firenzuola and the road down the Santerno valley. This was indeed a critical sector for the Germans, for it was one of the few areas on the northern slopes of the mountains where any quantity of artillery and transport could be deployed once over the watershed.

By September 27 Clark's infantry had fought its way forward to within ten miles of Route 9 at Imola, before being halted by fierce and co-ordinated counter-attacks by no less than four German divisions. In attempting to recapture Monte Battaglia, Kesselring threw in units from many divisions, including some pulled out from the Adriatic front, against the U.S. 88th Division. The battle lasted for over a week before the exhausted German infantry was ordered to dig in. But with mounting casualties and deteriorating weather, Clark also called a halt and turned his attention to Route 65, which would lead him to Bologna.

Coriano ridge taken

On the 8th Army front the Canadians and V Corps resumed the offensive on the night of September 12 and drove the Germans off the Coriano and Gemmano ridges, but it took the Canadians three whole days of bitter and costly fighting to clear San Fortunato. On September 20, Rimini fell to the 3rd Greek Mountain Brigade, who fought well in this its first engagement, and the following day Allied patrols were across the Marecchia. Now, as Freyberg's 2nd New Zealand Division passed through on Route 16, the rivers were filling and near spate and the heavy soil of the Romagna was beginning to grip both men and vehicles as they struggled forward. The Romagna is an immense flat expanse of alluvial soil carried down by a dozen or so rivers and innumerable smaller watercourses that discharge into the Adriatic. Reclaimed and cultivated over centuries, it is still essentially a swamp, criss-crossed by ditches and with the watercourses channelled between floodbanks that rise in places 40 feet above the plain. Moreover, the numerous stone-built farmhouses and hamlets, vineyards, and long rows of fruit trees afforded the defence ready-made strongpoints and cover. Inauspicious terrain indeed, with all the odds against a rapid advance. By the 29th only the leading elements of the New Zealand and 56th Divisions had reached the banks of the River Fiumicino and the Germans were still entrenched in the foothills south of Route 9. Torrential rain, however, brought all forward movement to a halt, sweeping away bridges and making fords impassable. But in the mountains X Corps still fought on and by October 8 was within ten miles of Cesena.

General Leese, who had been given command of the Allied Land Forces in South-East Asia, had now been succeeded by General Sir Richard McCreery. The new army commander, deciding to avoid the low ground, launched in succession the 10th Indian Division and the Poles through the mountains. And by October 21 Cesena had been taken and bridgeheads seized over the Savio. After resisting for four days the Germans voluntarily withdrew to the line of the Ronco.

Striking now towards Bologna, Clark's II Corps met growing resistance. Initially it had benefited from heavy air support, including strategic bombers, and the efforts of the 8th Army to break out along Route 9. It had been opposed by less than two divisions. By the time it reached the Livergano escarpment, however, it was faced by no less than five divisions (including the 16th S.S. Panzer Division), and elements from three other divisions. This was the work of von Senger, who was temporarily in command of the 10th Army owing to the illness of Lemelsen. Helped by a spell of fine weather, which gave the Allied air forces the chance to intervene, II Corps drove the Germans off the escarpment on October 14. But von Senger was bringing in more and more troops and had the defences of Bologna properly co-ordinated and well covered by artillery. Although the 88th Division captured Monte Grande on October 20, with the assistance of fighter-bombers and the expenditure of 8,600

∆ *American troops in Monghidoro.*

rounds of gun ammunition, the Americans were beaten back from the little village of Vedriano on three successive nights by fierce counter-attacks.

Since September 10, in just over six weeks II Corps had lost 15,716 men, and over 5,000 of these casualties had been in the 88th Division. On October 25, Clark gave the order to dig in. He himself chose to share some of the discomforts of his men and proposed to sit the winter out in his caravan near the Futa pass, one of the highest parts of the Apennines.

∇ *Bailey bridge at Vergato, named after the late president of the United States.*

On the other flank, the 8th Army's operations were similarly halted; the weather had broken completely and both sides were exhausted. Alexander wrote that "the rain, which was at that time spoiling Fifth Army's attack on Bologna, now reached a high pitch of intensity. On 26th October all bridges over the Savio, in our immediate rear, were swept away and our small bridge heads over the Ronco were eliminated and destroyed."

Since August the Germans had lost 8,000 prisoners, and LXXVII Panzer Corps alone had suffered over 14,500 battle casualties. Over a third of Kesselring's 92 infantry battalions were down to 200 men each and only ten mustered over 400. In the 8th Army, battle casualties since July totalled 19,975, and every infantry battalion had to be reorganised. Tank casualties were well over 400 and the 1st Armoured Division had to be disbanded.

Winter war

In north-west Europe all chances of a decisive victory over Nazi Germany in 1944 ended with the reverse at Arnhem and the delay in opening the port of Antwerp. A winter campaign was now inevitable. In Italy, Kesselring's Operation *"Herbstnebel"* (Autumn Fog), to shorten his line by withdrawing to the Alps, was peremptorily turned down by Hitler. Alexander's long-term proposal for an enveloping attack by landing in Yugoslavia could make no immediate contribution to Eisenhower's present predicament and indeed proved to be a pipe dream that for political reasons alone would never have been authorised. So it was the mixture as before, with Hitler still obsessed with the Balkans, Kesselring

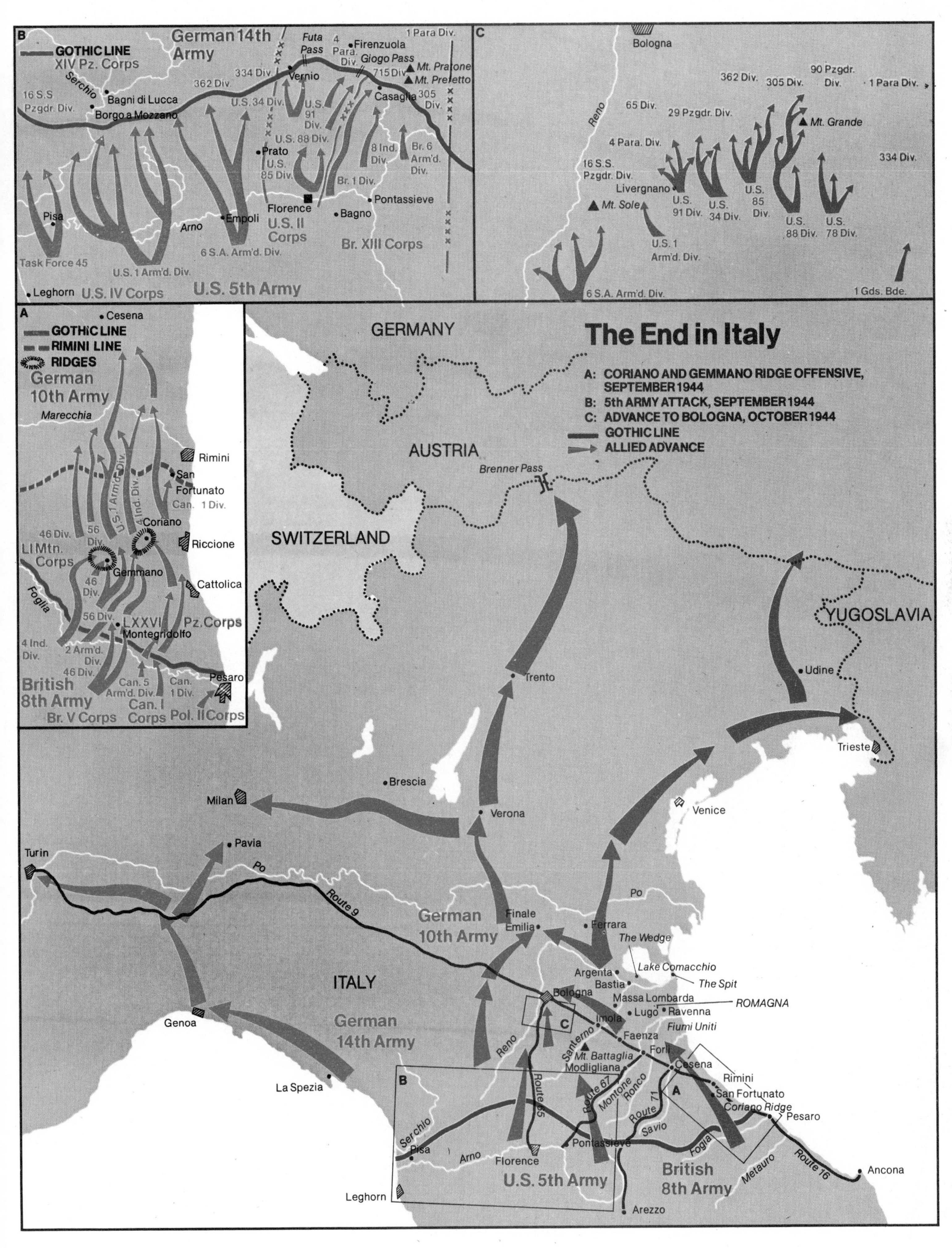

The End in Italy
A: CORIANO AND GEMMANO RIDGE OFFENSIVE, SEPTEMBER 1944
B: 5th ARMY ATTACK, SEPTEMBER 1944
C: ADVANCE TO BOLOGNA, OCTOBER 1944
GOTHIC LINE
ALLIED ADVANCE
GERMANY
AUSTRIA
SWITZERLAND
YUGOSLAVIA
ITALY
Brenner Pass
Trento
Udine
Trieste
Brescia
Milan
Verona
Venice
Turin
Pavia
Po
Route 9
German 10th Army
German 14th Army
Finale Emilia
Ferrara
The Wedge
Lake Comacchio
The Spit
Argenta
Bastia
Bologna
Massa Lombarda
ROMAGNA
Lugo
Ravenna
Fiumi Uniti
Imola
Faenza
Forlì
Cesena
Rimini
San Fortunato
Coriano Ridge
Pesaro
Mt. Battaglia
Modigliana
Santerno
Reno
Route 65
Route 67
Montone
Ronco
Route 71
Savio
Foglia
Metauro
Route 16
Ancona
Genoa
La Spezia
Serchio
Pisa
Arno
Florence
Pontassieve
Leghorn
Arezzo
U.S. 5th Army
British 8th Army
B
GOTHIC LINE
German 14th Army
XIV Pz. Corps
Futa Pass
Firenzuola
1 Para Div.
4 Para. Div.
Giogo Pass
715 Div.
Mt. Pratone
Mt. Prefetto
334 Div.
Vernio
362 Div.
16 S.S. Pzgdr. Div.
Bagni di Lucca
Borgo a Mozzano
U.S. 34 Div.
U.S. 91 Div.
Casaglia
305 Div.
U.S. 88 Div.
Prato
U.S. 85 Div.
8 Ind. Div.
Br. 6 Arm'd. Div.
Br. 1 Div.
Pontassieve
Pisa
Empoli
Florence
Bagno
U.S. II Corps
Br. XIII Corps
Arno
6 S.A. Arm'd. Div.
Task Force 45
U.S. 1 Arm'd. Div.
Leghorn
U.S. IV Corps
U.S. 5th Army
C
Bologna
362 Div.
305 Div.
90 Pzgdr. Div.
1 Para Div.
65 Div.
29 Pzgdr. Div.
Mt. Grande
4 Para. Div.
16 S.S. Pzgdr. Div.
334 Div.
Livergnano
U.S. 91 Div.
U.S. 34 Div.
U.S. 85 Div.
U.S. 88 Div.
U.S. 78 Div.
Mt. Sole
U.S. 1 Arm'd. Div.
6 S.A. Arm'd. Div.
1 Gds. Bde.
A
Cesena
GOTHIC LINE
RIMINI LINE
RIDGES
German 10th Army
Marecchia
Rimini
San Fortunato
Can. 1 Div.
U.S. 1 Arm'd. Div.
4 Ind. Div.
Coriano
46 Div.
56 Div.
Riccione
LI Mtn. Corps
Gemmano
Cattolica
Foglia
56 Div.
LXXVI Pz. Corps
Montegridolfo
4 Ind. Div.
2 Arm'd. Div.
46 Div.
Pesaro
British 8th Army
Can. 5 Arm'd. Div.
Can. 1 Div.
Br. V Corps
Can. I Corps
Pol. II Corps

over-sensitive of his coastal flank on the Adriatic, but ordered to fight where he stood, and Alexander with dwindling resources committed to a continuation of the battle of attrition against the grain of the country and in the most adverse climatic conditions. Furthermore, the bad weather was seriously limiting the use of Allied air power, at a time when the Allies were facing a world-wide shortage of certain types of artillery ammunition as a result of the extraordinarily sanguine and premature decision to set back production.

The fighting continued until early January, with the Allies aiming to reach Ravenna and break the line of the Santerno before reviewing the thrust to Bologna. In the north "Ponterforce",

consisting of Canadian and British armoured units and named after its commander, co-operating with "Popski's Private Army" of desert fame, reached the banks of the Fiumi Uniti and Ravenna itself fell to I Canadian Corps. Soon the Canadians reached the southern tip of Lake Comacchio, but it was only after a fierce and costly battle that they were able to force the Germans back behind the line of the Senio. Astride Route 9, attacking westwards, V Corps captured Faenza, and in the foothills south of the road the Poles fought forward to the upper reaches of the Senio. At this point the 5th Army was stood-to at 48 hours' notice on December 22 to resume the attack.

But the weather again broke and by a quirk of fate Mussolini, despised by friend and foe alike, and seeking a "spectacular" success for his newly formed divisions, made a last throw in a losing game. These two divisions, the "Monte Rosa" and the "Italia" Bersaglieri Divisions, led by the German 148th Division, now launched a counter-attack on the extreme left flank of the 5th Army. This advance towards the vital port of Leghorn came on the very day that virtually the whole of the 5th Army was concentrated and poised ready to attack Bologna. Only the 92nd (Negro) Division, posted around Bagni di Lucca, was in position to meet the attack down the wild and romantic valley of the Serchio. The arrival of 8th Indian Division on December 25 was only just in time to stop a complete breakthrough, as the leading German units overran the two main defence lines before being held and driven back by the Indians. Meanwhile this threat to the main supply base had caused two more of the 5th Army's divisions to be switched from the main battle area, and with heavy snow falling in the mountains, Alexander gave the order for both armies to pass to the defensive.

Command shuffles

During the winter months there were changes in command on both sides. On the death of Sir John Dill, head of the British mission to Washington, Maitland Wilson was sent in his place and Alexander became Supreme Allied Commander Mediterranean, with promotion to Field-Marshal, backdated to the capture of Rome. Clark now commanded the 15th Army Group, and Truscott was recalled from France to take over the 5th Army. On the German side Lemelsen still commanded the 14th Army and General Traugott Herr, whose corps had held the early attacks on the Adriatic flank, the 10th Army in what was to prove the critical eastern sector. Kesselring left in the middle of March to become O.B. West and Vietinghoff, hurriedly recalled from the Baltic, took his place with unequivocal orders from Hitler to hold every yard of ground. This further example of the Führer's inept "rigid defence" doctrine proved disastrous, as Vietinghoff entered the ring for the final round of the campaign like a boxer with his bootlaces tied together!

In conditions of heavy snow and frost, the struggle on both sides was now against the forces of nature, and the Allied supply routes could only be kept open by the daily and unremitting efforts of thousands of civilians and all but those units in the most forward positions. While the Germans hoarded their meagre supplies of petrol and both sides built up stocks of ammunition, the Allied units at last began to receive some of the specialised equipment they had for so long been denied; "Kangaroos", the Sherman tanks converted to carry infantry; D.D.s, the amphibious tanks that had swum ashore onto the Normandy beaches; and "Fantails", tracked landing vehicles for shallow waters, of which 400 were promised for use on Lake Comacchio and the nearby flooded areas. At the same time the armoured regiments were re-equipped with up-gunned Sherman and Churchill tanks, Tank-dozers, and "Crocodile" flame-throwing tanks, many of which were fitted with "Platypus" tracks to compete with the soft ground of the Romagna. Throughout the remaining winter months the "teeth" arms were busy training with new assault equipment, such as bridge-laying tanks and flame throwers. The experience of the British 78th Division, back after refitting in the Middle East, is a typical example of the hard work put into preparing for the spring offensive.

"Training began almost at once–exercises for testing communications, in river crossings, in street fighting and, above all in co-operation with armour. 2 Armoured Brigade . . . was affiliated to the Division for these exercises . . . it was the first time in Italy that 78 Division

△ ◁ In the British V Corps' rear area: men of the 8th Army get a chance to have a closer (and safer!) look at the armoured vehicles used by the Germans. Note the hoarding for the exhibition, featuring Jon's immortal "Two Types".
▽ ◁ British Churchill tanks in action in the artillery support rôle.
△ German prisoners in Italy.

▵ *S.S.* Obergruppenführer *Karl Wolff, military governor of northern Italy and Germany's liaison man with Mussolini. Realising that the war was lost, he negotiated an armistice with the Allies, effective from May 2, 1945.*
▹ *American liberation forces enter the city of Milan, led by an armoured car of the Italian Communist partisans.*
▿ *Knocked-out motor transport in Italy.*

had lived, trained, and held the line with the armour with which it was later to carry out full-scale operations: this was the genesis of the splendid team work between tanks and infantry soon to be shown in the final battle."

Before handing over, Kesselring kept his troops hard at work building defences on every river-line right back to the Reno and indeed on the line of the Po itself. Although milked of forces for the other fronts, his two armies still contained some of the very best German divisions. These were now well up to strength and fully rested, as for instance the two divisions of I Parachute Corps, commanded by the redoubtable General Richard Heidrich, which between them mustered 30,000 men. The active front, however, much of which was on difficult ground not of his own choosing, was 130 miles long, and his supply lines were constantly being attacked from the air and by partisans. To cover his front he allocated 19 German divisions (including the 26th Panzer, and 29th and 90th *Panzergrenadier).* Five more German infantry divisions, plus four Italian divisions and a Cossack division, were held back to watch the frontiers and, in particular, to guard against a landing in the Gulf of Venice. Here, had he but known, sand-bars precluded large-scale amphibious operations.

The relative strength of the 15th Army Group was now lower than ever before. Three divisions had been rushed to intervene in the civil war in Greece and I Canadian Corps had left for Holland in February. There remained only 17 divisions, including the newly arrived American 10th Mountain Division. But Alexander held an ace–overwhelming strength in the air. With the combined bomber offensive drawing to a close, more and more heavy bomber squadrons were released to support the coming offensive and by April were pounding away at the

German supply routes. By D-day every railway line north of the Po had been cut in many places. Nor had the two tactical air forces been idle. On February 6, 364 sorties were flown against the Brenner pass and targets in the Venetian plain, while in March the German supply dumps, so carefully built-up during the winter, were systematically attacked. Above the battlefield, in clearing skies, the Allies' planes roamed at will and when the offensive opened, a total of 4,000 aircraft was available to intervene directly in the land battle.

The last lap

Alexander's plan was again for a double-fisted attack, but with a bold and carefully set-up change of direction by the 8th Army at the very moment when the 5th Army was to deliver the second blow. Once again the Germans were to be misled into expecting a major landing (south of Venice) and realism was brought to this cover plan by the joint Commando/56th Division operations to clear the "spit" and "wedge", on the near shore, and the islands of Lake Comacchio, which in fact were vital to the real flanking thrust inland. Meanwhile the whole of the 8th Army, except for a skeleton force in the mountains, was secretly concentrated to the north of Route 9. On 9 April, V Corps (8th Indian and 2nd New Zealand Divisions) and the Polish II Corps would open the offensive across the River Senio astride Lugo, with the object of seizing bridgeheads over the Santerno and exploiting beyond. At this point the 5th Army would attack towards Bologna, while the 56th Division would cross Lake Comacchio in "Fantails" and the 78th Division would debouch from the Santerno bridgeheads and strike northwards to Bastia. This change of axis by the 8th Army aimed at breaking the "hinge" of the whole German position at Argenta and cutting their lines of withdrawal eastwards.

Shortly after mid-day on April 9, the Allied air forces went to work with the medium bombers and close support squadrons attacking command posts, gun positions, and strongpoints on the Senio and beyond, while in an hour and a half the heavy bombers, using a line of smoke shells in the sky as a bomb line, saturated the German defences on the immediate

The end of the road for Hitler's armies in Italy.
△ *Prisoners taken by the U.S. IV Corps await transfer to a prisoner-of-war camp and, in the long run, repatriation to Germany.*
▷ *British troops with prisoners.*

front of the two assault corps with 125,000 fragmentation bombs. This deluge of bombs was immediately followed by four hours of concentrated gun and mortar fire, alternating with low-level fighter-bomber attacks. At 1900 hours as the last shells burst on the forward defences, the fighter-bombers swept over in a dummy attack to keep the enemy's heads down until the infantry crossed the river. Within minutes the first flame-throwers were in action and "the whole front seemed to burst into lanes of fire". Overnight there was bitter fighting before the western flood banks were breached and bridges laid for the armour and anti-tank guns to cross. The next day over 1,600 Allied heavy bombers renewed their attack, and on the third day of the offensive the New Zealanders were across the Santerno at Massa Lombarda. The German 98th and 362nd Divisions had lost over 2,000 prisoners and their forward battalions had been virtually destroyed.

Meanwhile the battle for the Argenta Gap had started. The 78th Division, having crossed the Santerno, was advancing rapidly, led by a special striking force (the Irish Brigade and 2nd Armoured Brigade) of all arms, part of which was entirely mounted on tracked vehicles, and which became known as the "Kangaroo Army". The approaches to Bastia, however, were covered by thousands of mines and the Germans fought to the last round, while in crossing Lake Comacchio, the 58th Division suffered heavy casualties. But slowly the pincer attacks closed on Argenta itself and McCreery's reserve divisions began to move up.

Now was the time for Truscott to launch his two corps, but poor flying conditions delayed the attack until April 14. Over the next four days the Allied air forces

▷ *Lieutenant-General Frido von Senger und Etterlin discusses the terms for the surrender of the German forces in Italy with Major-General Gruenther in Caserta.*

▽ *The scene outside Milan Cathedral after the liberation of the city.*

flew over 4,000 sorties in support and in the first 30 minutes of the attack on Monte Sole and the nearby Monte Rumici, 75,000 shells fell on the German mountain strongpoints. In three days' fighting the U.S. II Corps was held down and advanced less than two miles. West of Route 64, however, the 10th Mountain Division captured Montepastore and for two days the U.S. 1st Armoured Division and the 90th *Panzergrenadier* Division, Vietinghoff's last reserve, fought it out in the valley of the Samoggia. Suddenly the end was within sight. Around Argenta the 29th *Panzergrenadier* Division and the remnants of a number of other divisions kept up a bitter struggle to prevent a breakthrough by the 6th Armoured Division, but by April 20 V Corps' leading columns were within 15 miles of Ferrara, advancing on a broad front. Along Route 9 the New Zealanders and Poles had fought three German divisions to a standstill and at dawn on April 21 a Polish brigade entered Bologna unopposed. The previous day a company of the U.S. 86th Mountain Infantry was across Route 9, west of the city, and now Truscott's II Corps, with the 6th South African Armoured Division, swept past on Route 64. On April 23 the leading tanks made contact with a squadron of 16th/5th Lancers, 15 miles west of Ferrara.

On April 20, Vietinghoff, in defiance of Hitler's demands, ordered a withdrawal to the Po, but the fate of his armies was already sealed. What was left of his shattered units was trapped against the Po, where every bridge was down or blocked by packed columns of burning vehicles. Von Senger was amongst those who succeeded in crossing. "At dawn on the 23rd we found a ferry at Bergantino; of the thirty-six Po ferries in the zone of Fourteenth Army, only four were still serviceable. Because of the incessant fighter-bomber attacks it was useless to cross in daylight."

When the Allied armoured columns crossed 36 hours later, they left behind them "a scene of extraordinary desolation and fearful carnage. There was no longer any coherent resistance, and along the river lay the ruins of a German army." In the first 14 days of the offensive the German casualties were around 67,000, of whom 35,000 had been taken prisoner. Allied casualties were a little over 16,500. On May 2 the remaining German and Italian troops of Army Group "C", nearly a million men, surrendered.

The American Douglas A-20G Havoc attack bomber

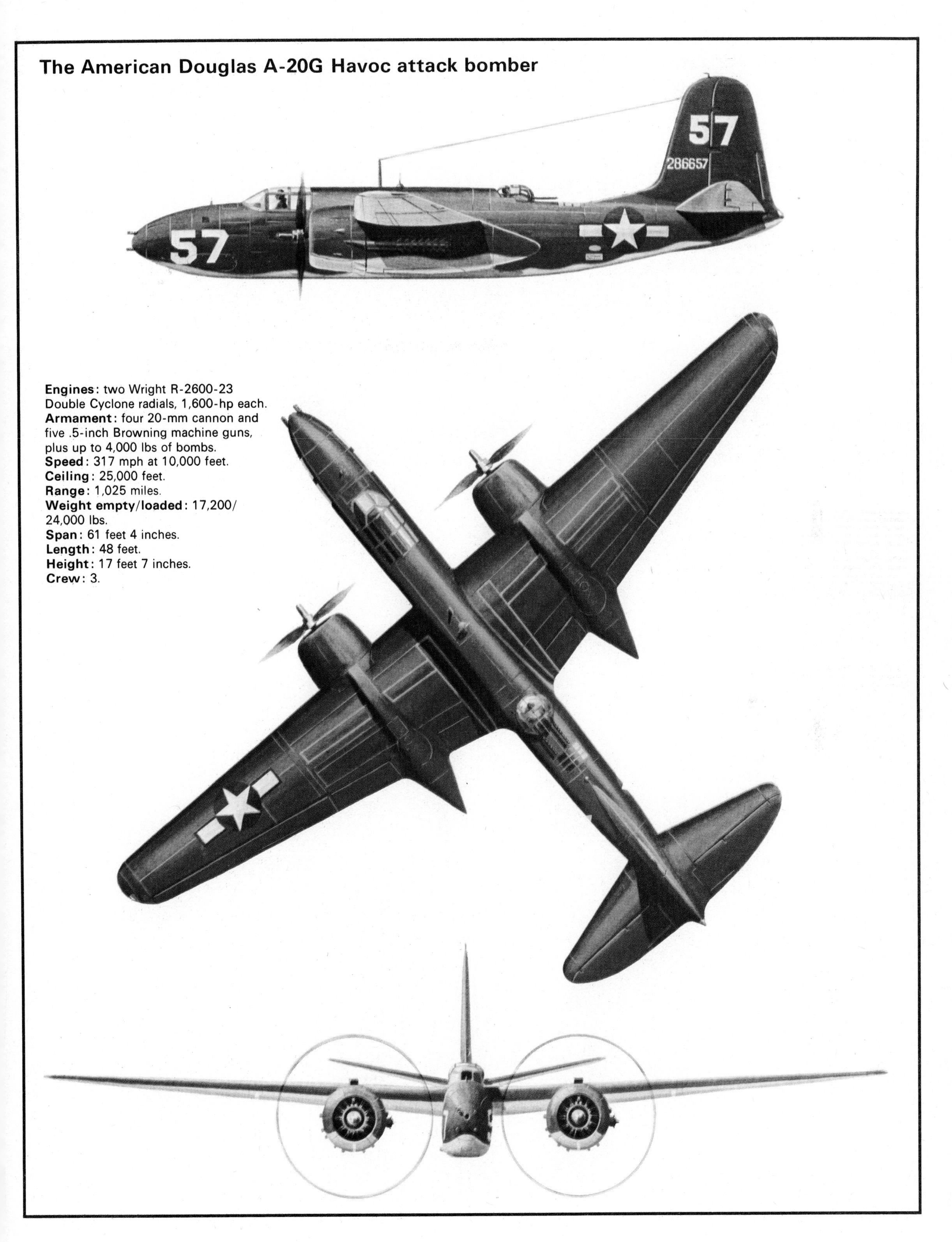

Engines: two Wright R-2600-23 Double Cyclone radials, 1,600-hp each.
Armament: four 20-mm cannon and five .5-inch Browning machine guns, plus up to 4,000 lbs of bombs.
Speed: 317 mph at 10,000 feet.
Ceiling: 25,000 feet.
Range: 1,025 miles.
Weight empty/loaded: 17,200/ 24,000 lbs.
Span: 61 feet 4 inches.
Length: 48 feet.
Height: 17 feet 7 inches.
Crew: 3.

THE DEATH OF MUSSOLINI

After his rescue from the Gran Sasso by Otto Skorzeny on September 12, 1943, Mussolini met Hitler. Together the two leaders decided on the establishment of a new Fascist republic in what was left of Italy, and Mussolini's new government met at La Rocca on September 27. The German leader had no intention, however, of letting Mussolini's government actually run the country and refused to answer letters on the subject. The Fascist régime did manage to try some of those responsible for the July 1943 coup that ousted Mussolini. One of those found guilty and executed was Ciano. Opposition to the régime was growing, however, and in the middle of 1944 it was estimated that over 80,000 partisans were operating against the Fascists and Nazis.
With the final Allied victory imminent, Mussolini left for Como, where he was joined by his mistress, Clara Petacci.

◁◁ Mussolini's last days: the Duce inspects Fascist militia in Milan. There is little of his earlier swagger left in the "Caesar of the new Roman Empire".
▽ ◁ Arrested by Italian partisans on April 26, Mussolini and Clara Petacci were shot down without ceremony on the 28th in the small town of Dongo, near Como. The bodies of Mussolini, Petacci, and other Fascist leaders were then taken to Milan and dumped in the Piazza Loretto, where this photograph was taken.
◁ The mutilated bodies of Benito Mussolini and Clara Petacci.
▽ After lying in the street for several hours, the bodies were hung from the framework of a garage for the edification of the crowd. Mussolini is third from left and Petacci fourth.

CHAPTER 149

GERMANY: The trap closes

One of General Bradley's tasks was to reduce the "fortified area of the Ruhr" where, on Hitler's orders, Field-Marshal Model had shut himself in. Given the job of carrying out the operation, the American 15th Army attacked southwards across the Ruhr and westwards across the Sieg.

By April 12, Lieutenant-General Gerow had occupied the entire coal basin in which, despite the *Führerbefehl* of March 19, the Germans had done nothing to add to the destruction wrought by British and American bombing. Two days later, the pocket had been cut in two from north to south. In these conditions, Colonel-General Harpe, commanding the 5th *Panzerarmee,* recognising the fact that his chief had disappeared, ordered Army Group "B" to cease fighting. Capitulation delivered 325,000 prisoners (including 29 generals) into Allied hands. A vain search was instituted for Field-Marshal Hans Model, and it was learnt only four months later that he had committed suicide on April 21, lest he be handed over to the Russians after his surrender, and had been buried in a forest near Wuppertal.

Without waiting for the outcome here, the American 9th, 1st, and 3rd Armies exploited their advance to the full. Resis-

▽ *American infantry press on into Germany past an enormous concrete air raid shelter in Aix-la-Chapelle. Parked in the lee of the building is a Sherman tank.*

tance grew weaker every day, and the average daily haul of prisoners rose from 10,600 between February 22 and March 31 to 29,000 for the week April 2 to 9, and reached 50,000 in the middle of the month. Evidently, the *Landser* (German "Tommy") was at the end of his tether, in spite of the growing wave of drumhead courts martial and summary executions. In the heart of the Reich, the multiplication of divisions went on almost to the final day, but whether they belonged to the Wehrmacht or to the *Waffen*-S.S., these new divisions, *Panzergrenadier* for the most part, revealed the paucity of their training as soon as they came under fire.

The *Volkssturm,* which was intended to fill the gaps in defence, was a pitiful ragbag of middle-aged men and adolescents, armed and equipped with any weapon that came to hand. Witness the battalion leader, taken prisoner by the Canadian Army, who confided to Major Shulman:

"'I had 400 men in my battalion,' he said, 'and we were ordered to go into the line in our civilian clothes. I told the local Party Leader that I could not accept the responsibility of leading men into battle without uniforms. Just before commitment the unit was given 180 Danish rifles, but there was no ammunition. We also had four machine-guns and 100 anti-tank bazookas (Panzerfaust). None of the men had received any training in firing a machine-gun, and they were all afraid of handling the anti-tank weapon. Although my men were quite ready to help their country, they refused to go into battle without uniforms and without training. What can a Volkssturm man do with a rifle without ammunition! The men went home. That was the only thing they could do.'"

In these conditions, allowing for sporadic but short-lived retaliation here and

∇ An American 9th Army infantryman shelters behind a blasted tree as a road mine is exploded. Note the Sherman flail tank on the right, waiting to go into action. The sloping box at its rear contains chalk dust to mark the path cleared.
▷ American soldiers examine a Messerschmitt Me 262 fighter-bomber found in the outskirts of a wood. Note the 20-mm cannon shells in the foreground.
∇▷ Two soldiers with their families surrender to the British.

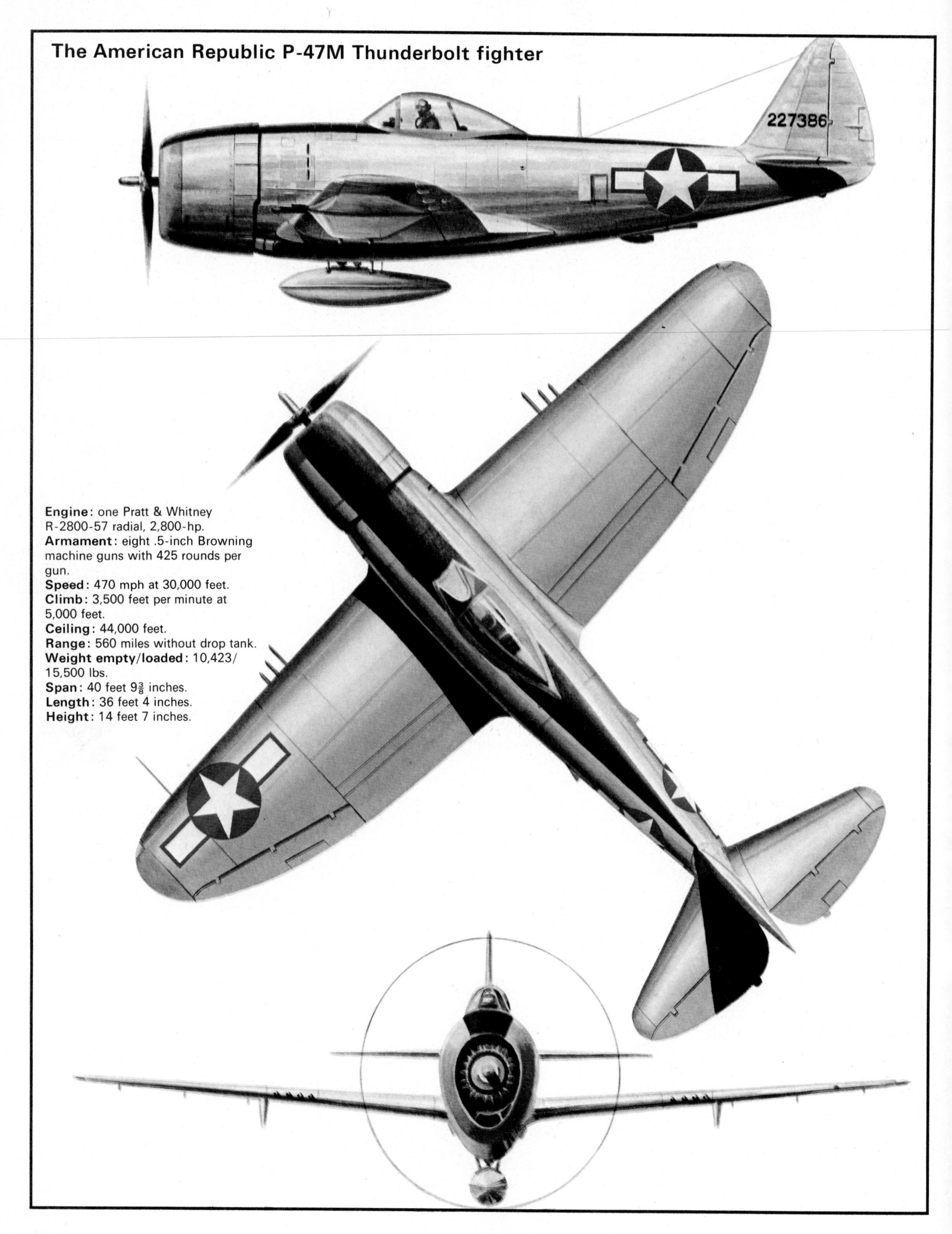

The American Republic P-47M Thunderbolt fighter

Engine: one Pratt & Whitney R-2800-57 radial, 2,800-hp.
Armament: eight .5-inch Browning machine guns with 425 rounds per gun.
Speed: 470 mph at 30,000 feet.
Climb: 3,500 feet per minute at 5,000 feet.
Ceiling: 44,000 feet.
Range: 560 miles without drop tank.
Weight empty/loaded: 10,423/15,500 lbs.
Span: 40 feet 9⅜ inches.
Length: 36 feet 4 inches.
Height: 14 feet 7 inches.

there from a few units that still retained some semblance of order and strength, the advance of the 12th Army Group across Germany gathered speed and took on more and more the character of a route march, facilitated by the *Autobahn* system, which in by-passing the towns removed inevitable bottlenecks. As a result, American losses dropped to insignificant figures. In the 3rd Army, according to Patton's record, for three corps of 12, then 14, divisions, between March 22 and May 8, 1945, they amounted to 2,160 killed, 8,143 wounded, and 644 missing, under 11,000 in all, compared with nearly 15,000 evacuated because of sickness and accidental injury.

On the left of the 12th Army Group, the American 9th Army, straddling the *Autobahn* from Cologne to Frankfurt-am-Oder to the south of Berlin, thrust towards Hannover, which it took on April 10, and three days later reached Wolmirstedt on the left bank of the Elbe, 85 miles further east. With the capture of Barby, slightly upstream of Magdeburg, it established a first bridgehead on the right bank of the river, thus putting its 83rd Division (Major-General R. C. Macon) some 75 miles from the New Chancellery. But then it turned instead towards Dessau and made contact there with the 6th Armoured Division (Major-General G. W. Read), which was moving ahead of the 1st Army.

The 1st Army had crossed the Weser at Münden and driven across Thuringia on a line linking Göttingen, Nordhausen, and Eisleben, covering nearly 80 miles between April 8 and 12. As has been mentioned above, it was its left flank that made contact with the 9th Army's right. This pincer movement cut off the retreat of the German 11th Army, which had stayed in the Harz mountains as ordered. To clear a way through for withdrawal, O.K.W. sent the *"Clausewitz"* Panzer Division to the rescue. It attacked at the junction between the 21st and 12th Army Groups and inflicted some damage on the 9th Army. But having got 35 to 40 miles from its point of departure, in the region of Braunschweig, it too was enveloped and annihilated. The same fate struck the 11th Army, falling almost to a man into Allied hands.

In the centre of the 1st Army, VIII Corps, after reaching the Elbe, managed to establish a bridgehead at Wittenberg, while to its right, VII Corps took Halle and Leipzig on April 14. The capture of Leipzig was a combined effort with the 9th Armoured Division, from the 3rd Army. In accordance with his instructions, General Hodges waited for some days on the Mulde, and it was only on April 26 at Torgau that he met up with Colonel-General Zhadov, commanding the Soviet 5th Guards Army. In the course of this rapid advance the 1st Army came across 300 tons of *Wilhelmstrasse* archives deposited in various places in the Harz. At Nordhausen, it occupied the vast underground factories where most of the V-1 and V-2 missiles were manufactured.

On March 30 the impetuous Patton was on the Werra and the Fulda. On April 12, the 3rd Army, changing its direction from north-east to east, crossed the Saale at Naumburg, Jena, and Saalfeld, having broken the last serious resistance offered by the enemy at Mühlhausen in Thuringia. And on April 7 the 3rd Army took the 400,000th prisoner since its campaign opened. On the 21st following, XX Corps reached Saxony and the vicinity of Chemnitz, VIII Corps reached a point beyond Plauen, while XII Corps, changing course from east to south-east, had got well beyond Bayreuth in Bavaria. This was the last exploit by Manton S. Eddy

▵ *Germany* in extremis: *bombed mercilessly, short of food, and without motor transport as a result of the fuel shortage. This is Darmstadt, which fell to the 26th Division of the U.S. 3rd Army.*
Overleaf top: *An unfortunate reminder of better days in shattered Rheydt–"What have you done for Germany today?"*
Overleaf bottom: *German civilians and their protection against stray bullets.*
Page 2359: *An American motor transport column, headed by a jeep, wends its way into Germany.*

who suffered a heart attack and had to hand over his corps to Major-General Stafford LeRoy Irwin. If the 1st Army had captured the *Wilhelmstrasse* archives, the 3rd discovered the last reserves of the *Reichsbank,* composed of gold bars worth 500,000,000 francs, small quantities of French, Belgian, and Norwegian currency and 3,000,000,000 marks in notes.

An ultimate regrouping by Bradley switched VIII Corps from Patton's command to Hodges's, and the progressive collapse of Army Group "B" permitted III and V Corps to be switched to the 3rd Army. Thus strengthened, it was given the assignment of supporting the activities of the 7th Army in Bavaria and upper Austria; specifically, to prevent the enemy establishing himself in the "national redoubt" zone, which General Strong, head of S.H.A.E.F. Intelligence, in a memorandum dated March 11, depicted as follows:

"Here, defended both by nature and by the most efficient secret weapons yet invented, the powers that have hitherto guided Germany will survive to reorganise her resurrection; here armaments will be manufactured in bombproof factories, food and equipment will be stored in vast underground caverns and a specially selected corps of young men will be trained in guerrilla warfare, so that a whole underground army can be fitted and directed to liberate Germany from the occupying forces."

Patton advanced with all speed, and on the day of the surrender he had pushed his XII Corps to a point ten miles below Linz on the Austrian Danube, and his III Corps, whose command had been taken over by Major-General James A. Van Fleet, as far as Rosenheim at the foot of the Bavarian Alps. On May 2, his 13th Armoured Division (Major-General Millikin) crossed the Inn at Braunau, birthplace of Adolf Hitler, who had just committed suicide in his bunker in the Berlin Chancellery.

Patton would have liked to complete his triumph by maintaining the drive of V (Major-General Clarence R. Huebner) and XII Corps as far as Prague. But on May 6, Eisenhower sent him categorical instructions via Bradley not to go beyond the Ceské Budejovice – Plzen – Karlovy Vary line in Czechoslovakia which he had reached. By this action, the Supreme Allied Commander, who had consulted Marshal Antonov, Stalin's Chief-of-Staff,

on the matter, yielded to the objections such an operation raised in the Soviet camp. In any event, the American 3rd Army met the spearhead of the 3rd Ukrainian Front, which had come up the Danube from Vienna, at Linz.

Montgomery drives for Lübeck

Montgomery's main task now was to push through to Lübeck and cut off the German forces occupying Norway and Denmark. He put the more energy and dispatch into the task knowing that its accomplishment would bring supplementary benefits:

"With the Rhine behind us we drove hard for the Baltic. My object was to get there in time to be able to offer a firm front to the Russian endeavours to get up into Denmark, and thus control the entrance to the Baltic."

For this purpose, he disposed of the British 2nd Army and the Canadian 1st Army, comprising five corps of 16 divisions (six of them armoured). Before him in Holland he found the German 25th Army, of which General von Blumentritt had just assumed command, and the debris of the 1st Parachute Army. This debilitated force had been put under the overall command of Field-Marshal Busch, who had been placed at the head of a Northern Defence Zone, to include the Netherlands, north-west Germany, Denmark, and Norway. Weakness in numbers and *matériel* was, however, to some extent offset by the fact that tracts of

▽ Stuttgart Cathedral, heavily damaged but still standing amidst the ruins of the rest of the city on March 31, 1945.

bog and the otherwise marshy nature of the ground kept the tanks to the main roads.

Having captured Münster, the key to Westphalia, General Dempsey, commanding the British 2nd Army, pushed forward his XXX Corps in the direction of Bremen, XII Corps towards Hamburg, and VIII Corps towards Lübeck.

On the right, VIII Corps (Lieutenant-General Sir Evelyn H. Barker) was momentarily delayed by the *"Clausewitz"* Panzer Division's counter-attack which, as has been mentioned above, was aimed at the point of contact of the 21st and 12th Army Groups. Nonetheless, VIII Corps reached the Elbe opposite Lauenburg on April 19. Here, Montgomery, anxious to move with all possible speed, requested support from Eisenhower and was given the U.S. XVIII Airborne Corps (8th Division, 5th and 7th Armoured Divisions, and the U.S. 82nd Airborne and British 6th Airborne Divisions). On April 29-30, British and Americans under cover provided by the first R.A.F. jet fighters, Gloster Meteors, forced the Elbe. On May 2, 11th Armoured Division (Major-General Roberts), which was the spearhead of the British VIII Corps, occupied Lübeck and the 6th Airborne Division entered Wismar, 28 miles further east, six hours ahead of Marshal Rokossovsky's leading patrols.

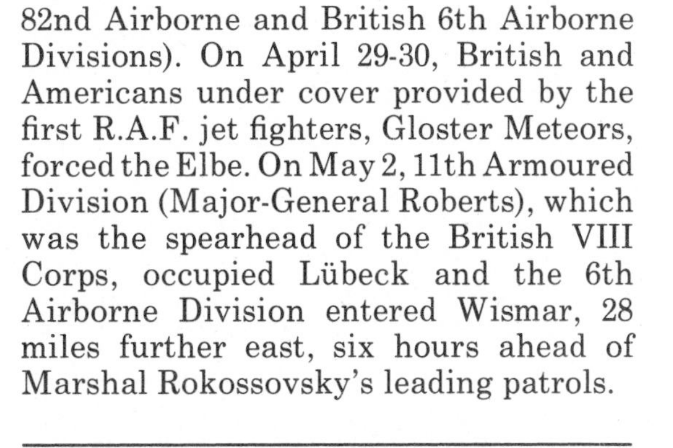

Hamburg and Bremen taken

XII Corps (Lieutenant-General Ritchie) had to sustain one last challenge on April 6 when crossing the Aller, a tributary on the right bank of the Weser. Afterwards, it took advantage of the bridgehead won on the Elbe by VIII Corps and closed in on Hamburg. On

▽ *Infantry of the 3rd Algerian Division cross the Lauter during their advance towards southern Germany and Austria.*

May 2, Lieutenant-General Wolz surrendered the ruins of the great Hanseatic port. Two days later, the 7th Armoured Division (Major-General Lyne) captured intact a bridge over the Kiel Canal at Eckernförde. Ritchie, who was within 35 miles of the town of Flensburg, where Grand-Admiral Dönitz had recently taken over the responsibilities of head of state, had brilliantly avenged the defeat inflicted on him at Tobruk.

In their drive on Bremen, Sir Brian Horrocks and his XXX Corps were held up by a great deal of destruction, and met with altogether fiercer resistance. Before Lingen, what was left of the 7th Parachute Division carried through a hand-to-hand counter-attack with frenetic *"Heil Hitler"* battle cries.

The 2nd *Kriegsmarine* Division showed the same aggressive spirit in defence, and it needed a pincer movement staged by three divisions to bring about the fall of Bremen on April 26. A few hours before the cease-fire, the Guards Armoured Division occupied Cuxhaven at the mouth of the Elbe.

Canadians in Holland

On April 1, General Crerar, commanding the Canadian 1st Army, recovered his II Corps, reinforced by the British 49th Division, thus bringing his divisions up to six. His mission was twofold: to drive between the Weser and the Zuiderzee with the British XXX Corps in the general direction of Wilhelmshaven and Emden; and to liberate the Dutch provinces still occupied by the enemy. The Canadian II Corps (Lieutenant-General Simonds), which had taken part in the crossing of the Rhine, fulfilled the first of these missions. On April 6, it liberated Zutphen and Almelo, and four days later Groningen and Leeuwarden. In this fine action, it was greatly helped by Dutch resistance while the French 2nd and 3rd Parachute Regiments dropped in the area of Assem and Meppel to open a way for it over the Orange Canal. On German territory, however, General Straube's II Parachute Corps put up a desperate fight, and Crerar had to call on Montgomery for help from the Polish 1st Armoured Division, the Canadian 5th Armoured Division, and the British 3rd Division. With this shot of new blood, the Canadian II Corps accelerated its advance and on May

△ An historic occasion: General Courtney Hodges, commander of the American 1st Army, greets Colonel-General A. S. Zhadov, commander of the Soviet 5th Guards Army, outside Togau on the Elbe on April 25. The Eastern and Western Allies had at last linked up, and Germany had been cut in two.

◁ The Möhne dam as the Americans found it in May 1945, rebuilt since the celebrated "dambuster" raid.

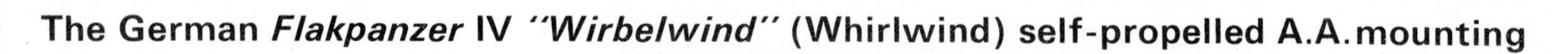

The German *Flakpanzer* IV *"Wirbelwind"* (Whirlwind) self-propelled A.A.mounting

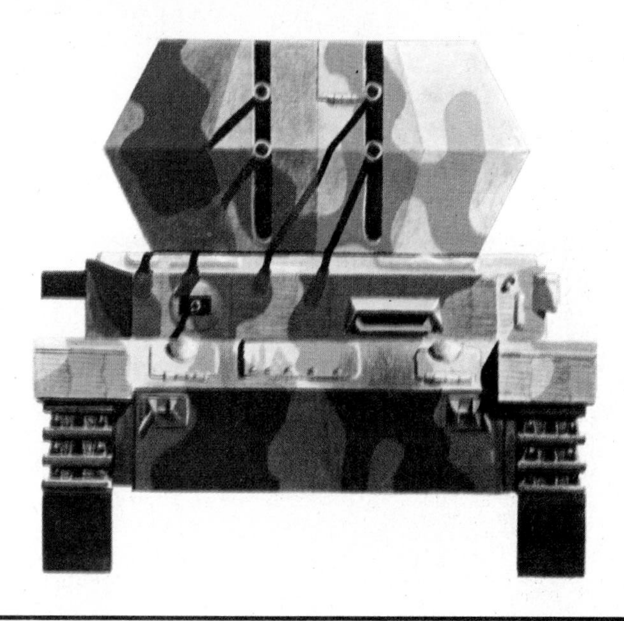

Weight: 25 tons.
Crew: 5.
Armament: one 2-cm *Flakvierling* 38 four-barrelled A.A. gun with 620 rounds.
Armour: hull front 85-mm, hull sides 30-mm, and turret 15-mm.
Engine: one Maybach HL 120 TRM inline, 300-hp.
Speed: 25 mph on roads and 10 mph cross-country.
Range: 125 miles on roads and 80 miles cross-country.
Length: 18 feet 9½ inches.
Width: 9 feet 4¾ inches.
Height: 8 feet 9½ inches.

5, 1945, General Maczek's Polish 1st Armoured Division was within nine miles of Wilhelmshaven, and the Canadian 5th Armoured Division on the outskirts of Emden.

The Canadian I Corps (Lieutenant-General C. Foulkes) took Arnhem by an outflanking movement and three days later reached the Zuiderzee at Harderwijk. The Germans responded to this attack by opening the sea-dykes, and Crerar, who was concerned to spare the Dutch countryside the ravages of flooding, agreed to a cease-fire with General von Blumentritt, stipulating in exchange that British and American aircraft be given free passage to provide the Dutch population with food and medical supplies. This dual operation cost the Canadian 1st Army 367 officers and 5,147 N.C.O.s and other ranks killed, wounded, and missing.

Last German high command change

While Field-Marshal Busch had been entrusted with the command of a "Northern Defence Zone", Kesselring was called upon to lead a "Southern Defence Zone" which included the German forces fighting between the Main and the Swiss frontier. So during the final phase of the campaign he found himself facing General Devers, whose 6th Army Group numbered 20 divisions on March 30, 1945, and 22 (13 American and nine French) the following May 8.

More French advances

The task of Lieutenant-General Patch and the American 7th Army was to cross the Rhine upstream of the 3rd Army, then having gained enough ground to the east, turn down towards Munich and make an assault on the "national redoubt", where, according to Eisenhower's Intelligence, Hitler would seek ultimate refuge. But there was no such mission in store for the French 1st Army which, in the initial plans, was ordered to send a corps over the Rhine, following the Americans, to operate in Württemberg, and later a division which would start off from Neuf-Brisach and occupy Baden-Baden.

△ *An armoured column of the American 3rd Army pushes over the border between Germany and Czechoslovakia. Patton, the army's commander, was typically impetuous in advancing far past his official stop line with "deep patrols".*

Neither General de Gaulle nor General de Lattre accepted this view of their intended mission. On March 4, de Gaulle remarked to de Lattre on "reasons of national importance that required his army to advance beyond the Rhine"; and de Lattre expounded the plan he had conceived to this end, which involved moving round the Black Forest via Stuttgart.

While de Gaulle worked on Eisenhower, de Lattre convinced General Devers of his point of view. The operation as conceived by de Lattre required possession of a section of the left bank of the Rhine below Lauterbourg; this was provided by the dexterity with which General de Monsabert managed to extend his II Corps from Lauterbourg to Speyer in the course of Operation "Undertone".

Patch moves south-east

On March 26, XV Corps of the American 7th Army managed without much trouble to cross the Rhine at Gernsheim below Worms. Patch exploited this success by taking Michelstadt then, turning south,

△ *A German tank factory, considerably damaged by U.S. heavy bombers and then overrun by American ground forces. Note the half-completed* Jagdpanther *tank destroyer on the left. Even though the Germans continued to step up the output of* matériel *right up to the end of the war, they did not have the fuel to make use of the weapons they already had.*

he took Mannheim and Heidelberg on March 30. On April 5, having moved up the Neckar as far as Heilbronn, he captured Würzburg in the Main valley. With his left as spearhead, he hurled his forces in the direction Schweinfurt–Bamberg–Nuremberg and on April 19, after some violent fighting, ended all resistance in Munich. With its right wing in contact with the French 1st Army in the Stuttgart area, and the left in touch with the American 3rd, the 7th Army moved in a south-easterly direction. On April 25, it crossed the Danube on an 80 mile front, capturing on the way what was left of XIII Corps with its commanding officer, Lieutenant-General Count d'Oriola.

Berchtesgaden taken

From that moment German resistance in Bavaria collapsed. On May 2, the American XV Corps occupied Munich. Two days later, the French 2nd Armoured Division, once more free for assignment with the Royan pocket liquidated, scaled the slopes of the Obersalzberg and occupied the Berghof, from which *Reichsmarschall* Hermann Göring had just fled. On the same day, the American 3rd Division, which had sped through Innsbruck, crossed the Brenner Pass and met up with the 88th Division of the American 5th Army at Vipiteno. On May 5, General Schulz, last commander of Army Group "G", avoiding capture by the French, surrendered at General Jacob L. Devers's H.Q.

On March 29, General de Gaulle telegraphed de Lattre: "It is essential that you cross the Rhine even if the Americans are against you doing so and even if you cross in boats. It is a matter of the highest national interest. Karlsruhe and Stutt-

gart are expecting you even if they don't want you."

When he received this message, de Lattre was on his way back from General Devers's H.Q. with the task of sending one corps, of at least three divisions (one of them armoured), across the Rhine to take Karlsruhe, Pforzheim, and Stuttgart. De Lattre had done all in his power to wring this order out of the army group commander. Pierre Lyautey remarks, on seeing him in the H.Q. of the Algerian 3rd Division on March 17, that he was in the process of conceiving "a great German campaign", which would be "full of Napoleonic dash and fury".

In any event, the 1st Army had ceded most of its bridging equipment to the 7th Army to compensate it for similar equipment made over to the 21st Army Group; in addition, in the afternoon of March 30, the French II Corps had barely completed the relief of the American VI Corps at Germersheim and Speyer. Nevertheless, Monsabert, who was down to about 50 motorised and unmotorised boats, was ordered to take two divisions across that very night.

The venture succeeded in conditions of apparently impossible improvisation,

△ *When the British arrived in Kiel they found the superb heavy cruiser* Admiral Hipper *there. She had spent the last months of her life supporting the army along the south coast of the Baltic Sea, but had then been heavily bombed in Kiel. She was scuttled in dock on May 3, 1945.*

Δ *An incongruous slogan in a town overrun by the Allies: "One People, one Reich, one Leader!"*

and in spite of resistance from the 47th *Volksgrenadier* Division, on March 31. By nightfall, the 3rd Algerian Division (General Guillaume), opposite Speyer, and the 2nd Moroccan Division (General Carpentier), opposite Germersheim, already had five battalions in Baden-Baden. The next day, the two bridgeheads were connected and the French advanced as far as the Karlsruhe–Frankfurt *Autobahn,* over 12 miles from the right bank. As for the 5th Armoured Division (General de Vernejoul), it crossed the Rhine either by ferrying or with the co-operation of General Brooks, commanding the U.S. VI Corps, "the perfect companion in arms" in de Lattre's words, over the American bridge at Mannheim. Finally, on April 2, the 9th Colonial Division, now under the command of General Valluy, crossed the river in its turn at Leimersheim (six miles south of Germersheim). Two days later, the 1st Army had taken its first objective, Karlsruhe.

As the German 19th Army was resisting fiercely in the Neckar valley and in the hills above Rastatt, making a stand in a strongly fortified position which covered the Baden-Baden plain, de Lattre shifted the weight of his thrust to the centre. This gave him Pforzheim on April 8, and he then sent his 2nd Moroccan Division, 9th Colonial Division, and 5th Armoured Division deep into the relative wilderness of the Black Forest. On April 10, the fall of Herrenalbon and the crossing of the Murg allowed Valluy to by-pass Rastatt and open the Kehl bridge to General Béthouart's I Corps.

In the meantime, Monsabert had seized Freudenstadt, the key to the Black Forest, and Horb on the Neckar above Stuttgart, while the American VI Corps was moving up on the capital of Württemberg by way of Heilbronn. On April 20, pushing on from Tübingen, the 5th Armoured Division completed the encirclement of the city. All resistance ceased after 48 hours. The French took 28,000 prisoners, what was left of the four divisions of LXIV Corps (Lieutenant-General Grimeiss).

The Stuttgart manoeuvre was the third act of this military tragedy, although by April 22, the fourth act, which saw the entrance of I Corps (4th Moroccan Division, 9th Colonial Division, 14th Division, and 1st Armoured Division), was well under way. Béthouart moved on Horb by way of Kehl and Oberkirch, where he turned south up the Neckar, reaching the Swiss frontier in the vicinity of Schaffhausen on the day Stuttgart fell. This led to the cutting off of XVIII S.S. Corps (General Keppler), which comprised four army divisions. These 40,000 Germans attempted to cut their way through the lines of the 4th Moroccan Mountain Division but they were taken in the rear by the 9th Colonial Division and on April 25 all resistance ceased.

The manoeuvre employed here by the 9th Colonial Division was the result of a request made by the Swiss High Command–as is told in the *History of the French 1st Army*–who were understandably not very enthusiastic about disarming and interning thousands of allegedly

△ *An aircraft factory in Hamburg, destroyed by R.A.F. Bomber Command.*

fanatical Germans. Although his plans were slightly put out by this development, de Lattre agreed:

"It is an obligation of another kind to give consideration to the permanent interests of Franco-Swiss friendship, especially when Switzerland, while keeping to its age old principle of neutrality, has always been faithful to this cause.

"The problem confronted me while Valluy was still about to attack the Kaiserstuhl and Lehr's combat command (5th Armoured Division) was still some hours away from Schaffhausen. But my hesitation was only momentary. I had no illusions as to the risks I ran but my inclination was on the side of Franco-Swiss comradeship. This inspired me to issue General Order No. 11 in the night April 20-21, ordering I Corps to 'maintain the drive of the right flank along the Rhine towards Basle, then Waldshut, with simultaneous action from Schaffhausen towards Waldshut so as to link up with the forces coming from Basle', hence ensuring the complete encirclement of the Black Forest and at the same time denying the S.S. divisions any opportunity to force the Swiss-German frontier."

In addition, the alacrity with which General Valluy tackled this new mission without the slightest warning deserves mention, Waldshut being not far short of 90 miles from the Kaiserstuhl via Lorrach.

The fifth and final act of the Rhine–Danube campaign involved the pincer movement carried out by Monsabert and Béthouart on Ulm, the one with the 5th Armoured Division and 2nd Moroccan Division (General de Linarès) to the north of the Danube, the other thrusting his 1st Armoured Division (General Sudre) south of the river along the line of Donaueschingen and Biberach. On April 24 at noon, the tricolour flew above the town which on October 21, 1805, had seen Mack surrender his sword to Napoleon. With the capture of Ulm a new pocket was established, and this yielded 30,000 prisoners.

On April 29, General de Lattre reformed I Corps, putting the 2nd Moroccan Division, the 4th Moroccan Mountain Division, and the 1st and 5th Armoured Divisions under its command, and giving it the task of destroying the German 24th Army, recently formed under General Schmidt with the object of preventing the French from gaining access into the Tyrol and Vorarlberg.

On the next day the 4th Moroccan Mountain Division (General de Hesdin) and the 5th Armoured Division, of which General Schlesser had just assumed command, captured Bregenz in Austria.

Once over the frontier, the French could count on the Austrian resistance to provide guides and information, leading in numerous instances to preventing planned demolition being carried out by the Wehrmacht. At Dornbirn the tanks of the 5th Armoured Division were bombarded with bouquets of lilac; at Bludenz, which was liberated on May 4, General Schlesser was made an honorary citizen. Meanwhile, the 2nd Moroccan Division and the 1st Armoured Division were moving beyond Ulm up the valley of the Iller; from Oberstdorf General de Linarès's Moroccan troops scaled the snow-covered slopes of the Flexenpass (5,800 feet). Nightfall on May 6 found them at Saint Anton, on the road to the Arlberg, having made contact with the American 44th Division on their left.

On May 7, at 1340 hours, a cease-fire was declared in Austria, following Kesselring's capitulation to General Devers. During its five weeks' campaign, the French 1st Army had brought total destruction on eight German divisions and taken 180,000 prisoners. Among these was Field-Marshal Rommel's son, whom de Lattre, with other considerations than victory in mind, generously released.

▽ Torpedoes that the Germans never had the chance to use. Although the menace of the conventional U-boat had been beaten by 1945, the Germans had high hopes of their new generation of fast Type XXI and XXIII boats. Post-war Allied evaluation of these new classes proved how dangerous such U-boats would have been.

CHAPTER 150

The Battle of Lake Balaton

Δ *The first Russian officer to enter Vienna poses in front of his Lend-Lease Sherman tank.*

In the meantime the German resistance had collapsed before the Red Army. The ring was closing round the New Chancellery in Berlin, and Vienna, the second capital of the Nazi Greater Germany, had been under Marshal Tolbukhin's control since April 13.

Between the Drava and the Carpathians, General Wöhler, commanding Army Group "South", had tried to break the Budapest blockade during the first fortnight of January. Although he had been reinforced by IV S.S. Panzer Corps, which had been withdrawn from East Prussia just before the Soviet attack on the Vistula, he failed in this attempt. The German 6th Army, which had just been transferred to General Balck's command, nevertheless managed to regain possession of the important military position of Székesfehérvár, but the effort exhausted its strength.

This setback sealed the fate of IX S.S. Mountain Corps, which, under the command of General Pfeffer-Wildenbruch, made up the Hungarian capital's garrison. On February 13, Buda castle, the defenders' last stronghold, fell to Marshal Malinovsky's troops (2nd Ukrainian Front), whilst the 3rd Ukrainian Front under Marshal Tolbukhin cleared Pest. The Russians claimed the Germans had lost 41,000 killed and 110,000 prisoners. The figures are certainly exaggerated, but nevertheless the 13th Panzer Division, the *"Feldherrnhalle" Panzergrenadier* Division, and the 33rd Hungarian S.S. Cavalry Division had been wiped out.

On March 6, the 6th *Panzerarmee*

△ *Colonel-General Heinz Guderian, architect of the German* Panzerwaffe, *a very competent field commander, and lastly the O.K.H. chief-of-staff. But as chief-of-staff he had the impossible task of trying to moderate the Führer's increasingly impossible military plans, and on March 28, 1945, he was replaced by Colonel-General H. Krebs.*
▷ *Hitler's last futile offensive, the battle of Lake Balaton.*
▷▷ *The Nazi machine attacked from within: two army officers hanged for having negotiated with the Russians in Vienna.*

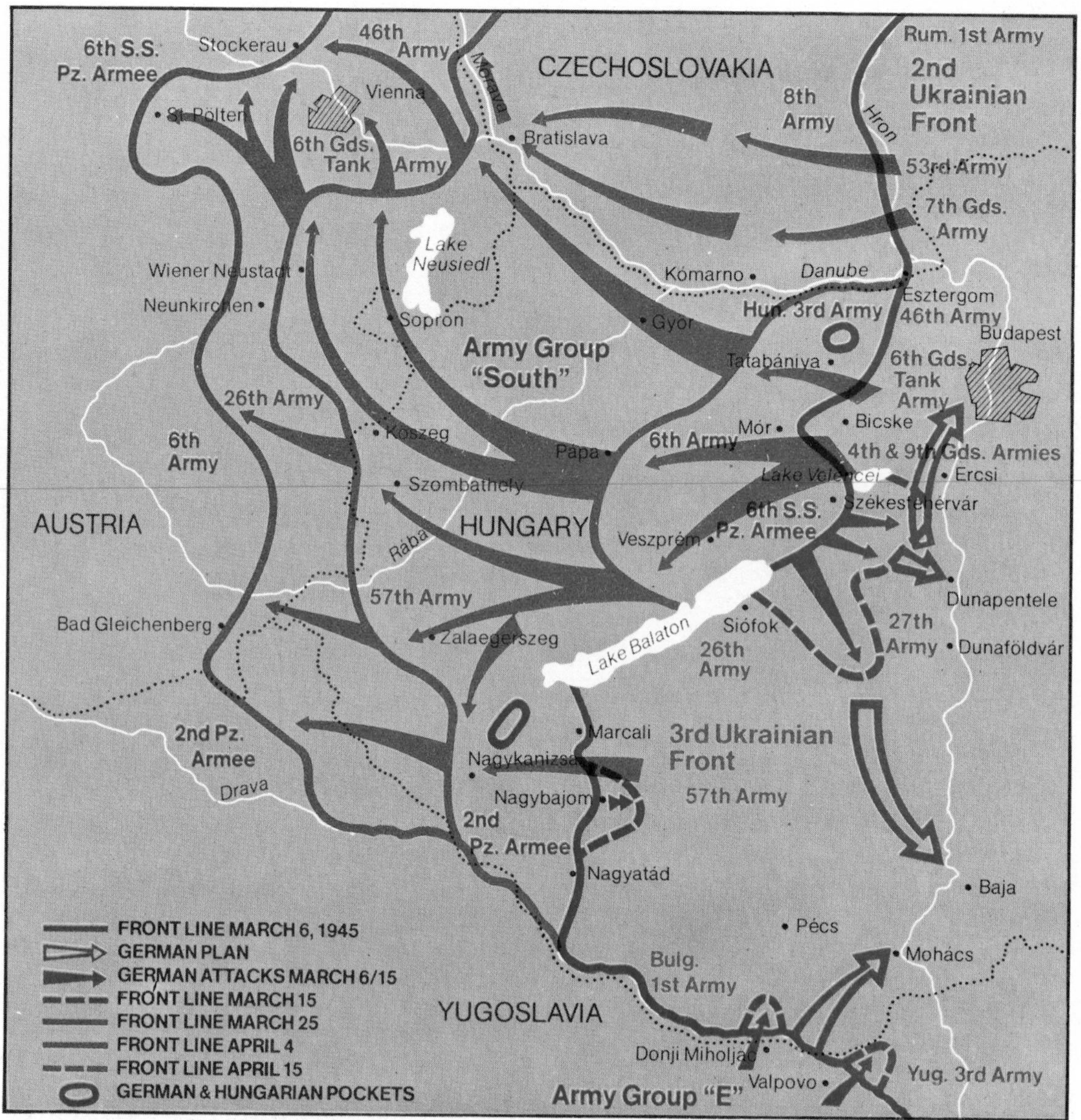

(Colonel-General Sepp Dietrich) went over to the offensive from the bastion of Székesfehérvár. Dietrich had left the Ardennes front on about January 25; it had taken six weeks for him to travel and take up his position. He might, on the other hand have reached the Oder front between February 5 and 10 if the plan that Guderian had vainly recommended to the Führer had been followed. The Führer in fact expected a miracle from this new offensive, indeed even the recapture of the Ploieşti oilfields.

The 3rd Ukrainian Front was to be smashed under the impact of a triple attack:

1. the left, the 6th *Panzerarmee,* consisting of eight Panzer (including the *"Leibstandarte Adolf Hitler", "Das Reich", "Hohenstaufen",* and *"Hitlerjugend"*), three infantry, and two cavalry divisions, was to deliver the main blow; it was to reach the Danube at Dunaföldvar and exploit its victory towards the south, with its left close to the Danube, its right on Lake Balaton;
2. between Lake Balaton and the Drava, the 2nd *Panzerarmee* (General de Angelis: six divisions) would immobilise Tolbukhin by attacking towards Kaposzvár; and
3. on the right, Army Group "E" (Colonel-General Löhr), in Yugoslavia, would send a corps of three divisions across the Drava, and from Mohacs move to the Danube.

The offensive of March 6 therefore committed 22 German divisions, including 19 from Army Group "South", out of the 39 that General Wöhler had under his command at the time. But this tremendous effort was of no avail. On the Drava and south of Lake Balaton, the German attack collapsed after 48 hours. The outlook for the 6th *Panzerarmee* seemed better on the day the engagement started, as the Panzers, massed on a narrow front, succeeded in breaking through, but the poorly-trained infantry proved incapable of exploiting this brief success. Tolbukhin, on the other hand, had organised his forces in depth and countered with his self-propelled guns. In fact, on March 12, Dietrich was halted about 19 miles from his starting point, but about 16 miles from his Danube objective.

The Russian riposte

On March 16, Marshals Malinovsky and Tolbukhin in their turn went over to the attack from the junction point of their two Fronts. Malinovsky planned to drive the German 6th Army back to the Danube between Esztergom and Komárom, whilst Tolbukhin, driving north-west of Lakes Velencei and Balaton, intended to split at its base the salient made in the Soviet lines by the 6th *Panzerarmee*.

The 2nd Ukrainian Front's troops had the easier task and reached their first objective by March 21, cutting off four of the 6th Army's divisions.

Tolbukhin, on the other hand, met such firm resistance on March 16 and 17 from IV S.S. Panzer Corps, forming Balck's right, that the *Stavka* put the 6th Guards Tank Army at his disposal. However, because of Malinovsky's success, Wöhler took two Panzer divisions from the 6th *Panzerarmee* and set them against Malinovsky's forces. As the inequality between attack and defence became increasingly marked, Dietrich managed to evacuate the salient he had captured between March 6 and 12, and then on March 24 he brought his troops back through the bottleneck at Székesfehérvár. But what he saved from the trap was merely a hotchpotch of worn-out men with neither supplies nor equipment.

On March 27, the 6th Guards Tank Army was at Veszprém and Devecser, 35 and 48 miles from its starting point. On March 29, Tolbukhin crossed the Rába at Sárvár, and Malinovsky crossed it at Györ, where it meets the Danube. The Hungarian front had therefore collapsed; this was not surprising as Wöhler, who had no reserves, had had 11 Panzer divisions more or less destroyed between March 16 and 27.

On April 6 Hitler, consistent in his misjudgement, stripped Wöhler of command of Army Group "South" and gave it to Colonel-General Rendulic, whom he

The British Supermarine Spitfire XIVE fighter and fighter-bomber

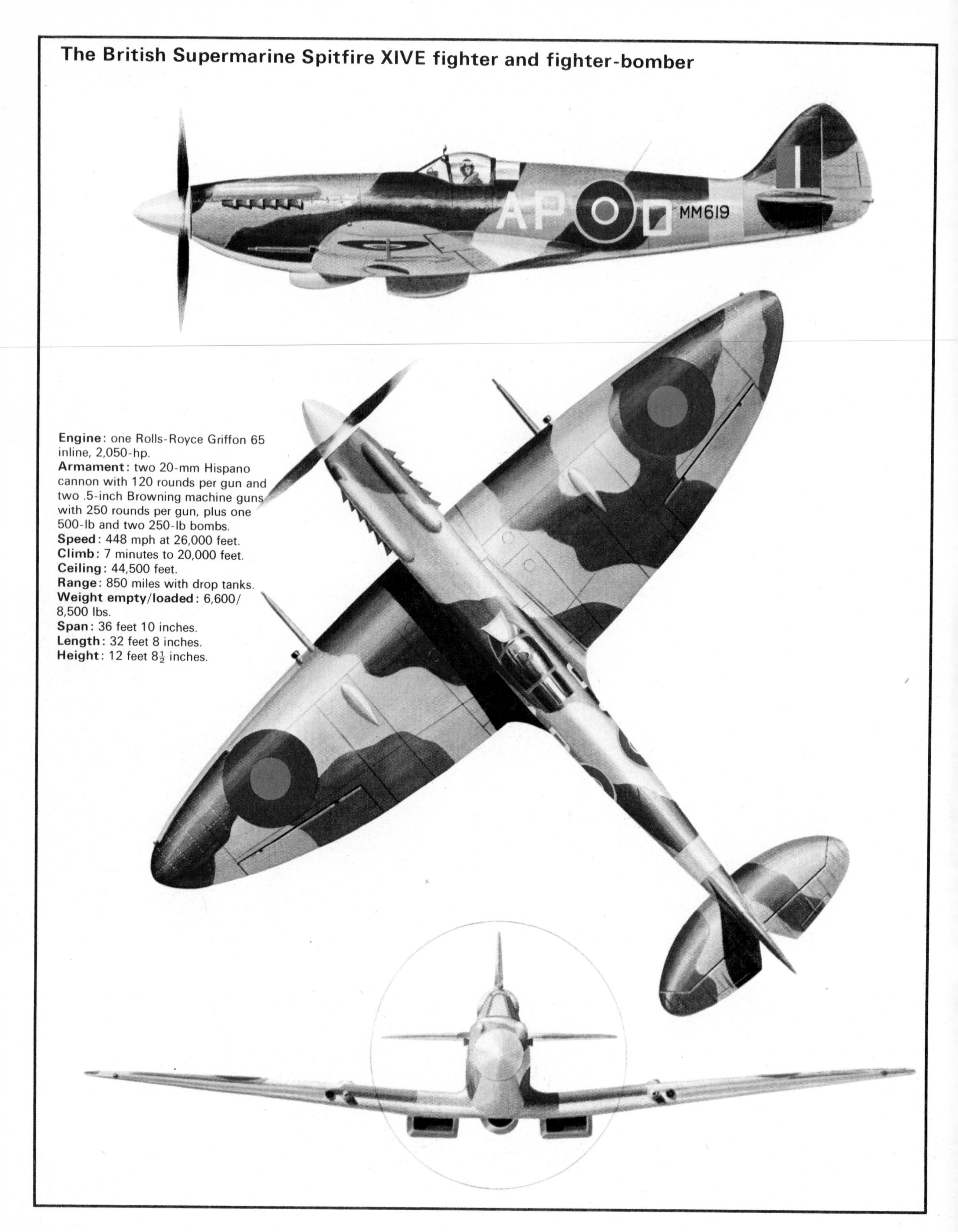

Engine: one Rolls-Royce Griffon 65 inline, 2,050-hp.
Armament: two 20-mm Hispano cannon with 120 rounds per gun and two .5-inch Browning machine guns with 250 rounds per gun, plus one 500-lb and two 250-lb bombs.
Speed: 448 mph at 26,000 feet.
Climb: 7 minutes to 20,000 feet.
Ceiling: 44,500 feet.
Range: 850 miles with drop tanks.
Weight empty/loaded: 6,600/ 8,500 lbs.
Span: 36 feet 10 inches.
Length: 32 feet 8 inches.
Height: 12 feet $8\frac{1}{2}$ inches.

recalled from the Kurland pocket for the task.

Vienna falls

But Malinovsky had already driven between Lake Neusiedl and the Danube on April 2, and had forced the Leitha at Bruck, whilst Tolbukhin, who had captured the large industrial centre of Wiener Neustadt, launched one column along the Semmering road towards Graz and another towards Mödling and Vienna. The day he took over his command, Rendulic was informed that the advance guard of the 3rd Ukrainian Front was already in Klosterneuburg north of Vienna, and that the 2nd Ukrainian Front was already approaching it from the south. A week later, a cease-fire was signed in the famous Prater Park, but in addition to the ordeal of a week's street fighting, the wretched Viennese still had to suffer much brutality and shameless looting from their "liberators".

Tolbukhin, who boasted of the capture of 130,000 prisoners, 1,350 tanks, and 2,250 guns, went up the right bank of the Danube, but his main forces did not go further than Amstetten, a small town 75 miles west of Vienna. On May 4, his patrols in the outskirts of Linz met a reconnaissance unit of the U.S. 3rd Army, and on the same day made contact with the advance guard of the British 8th Army on the Graz road. After helping to clear Vienna, Malinovsky sent his armies on the left across the Danube in the direction of Moravia. At Mikulov they crossed the pre-Munich (1938) Austro-Czechoslovak frontier. On the left bank of the Danube, the right wing of the 2nd Ukrainian Front, including the Rumanian 1st and 4th Armies (Generals Atanasiu and Dascalesco), liberated Slovakia and then, converging towards the north-west, occupied Brno on April 24 and were close to Olomouc when hostilities ceased. Slovakia's administration was handed over to the representatives of the Czechoslovak government-in-exile under Eduard Beneš as the occupation proceeded. On

▽ *Russian T-34/85 medium tanks move through an Austrian village in the closing days of the war.*

▵ *The Allies meet in Austria: Marshal of the Soviet Union F. I. Tolbukhin salutes General George S. Patton Jr.*

the other hand, Stalin seized Ruthenia in the lower Carpathian mountains; it had never even been a part of the Tsarist empire.

The defence of Berlin

On March 10, 1945, Hitler told Kesselring that he viewed the offensive Stalin was preparing to launch against Berlin with complete confidence. Colonel-General Guderian viewed the matter differently; urging Himmler to take soundings in Stockholm for surrender, he repeated several times: "It's not 11.55 now–it's 12.05!" In view of the open pessimism of his O.K.H. Chief-of-Staff, Hitler dismissed him on March 28 on grounds of ill health and appointed Colonel-General H. Krebs, who had been the German military attaché in Moscow on June 22, 1941, as his successor.

Army Group "Vistula" was charged with the defence of Berlin; Heinrich Himmler had just been replaced by Colonel-General Gotthard Heinrici, who rightly enjoyed the complete confidence of his staff and his troops. Cornelius Ryan's judgement seems quite correct:

"A thoughtful, precise strategist, a deceptively mild-mannered commander, Heinrici was nevertheless a tough general of the old aristocratic school who had long ago learned to hold the line with the minimum of men and at the lowest possible cost."

Heinrici was in contact with Army Group "Centre" a little below Guben on the Neisse, and was in control of the Oder front between Fürstenberg and Stettin, but the 1st Belorussian Front on both sides of Küstrin already had a wide bridgehead on the left bank of the river.

The German 9th Army, under General Busse, had the special mission of barring the invader's path to Berlin. It was accordingly deployed between Guben and the Hohenzollern Canal connecting the Oder and the Havel:

1. V S.S. Mountain Corps (337th, 32nd *"Freiwilligen"* S.S. Grenadier, and 236th Divisions) under General Jeckeln;
2. Frankfurt garrison of one division;
3. XI S.S. Panzer Corps (*"Müncheberg"* Panzer, 712nd, 169th, and 9th Parachute Divisions) under General M. Kleinheisterkamp;
4. XCI Corps (309th "Berlin", 303rd *"Döberitz"*, 606th, and 5th *Jäger* Division) under General Berlin.

This gave a total of 12 divisions on an 80 mile front. Busse, on the other hand, had kept the *"Kurmark"* Panzer Division in reserve on the Frankfurt axis and the 25th Panzer Division on the Küstrin axis.

The 3rd *Panzerarmee* was deployed between the Hohenzollern and Stettin canal; on a 95-mile front it had about ten divisions incorporated in XLVI Panzer Corps, XXXII Corps, and the 3rd Marine Division.

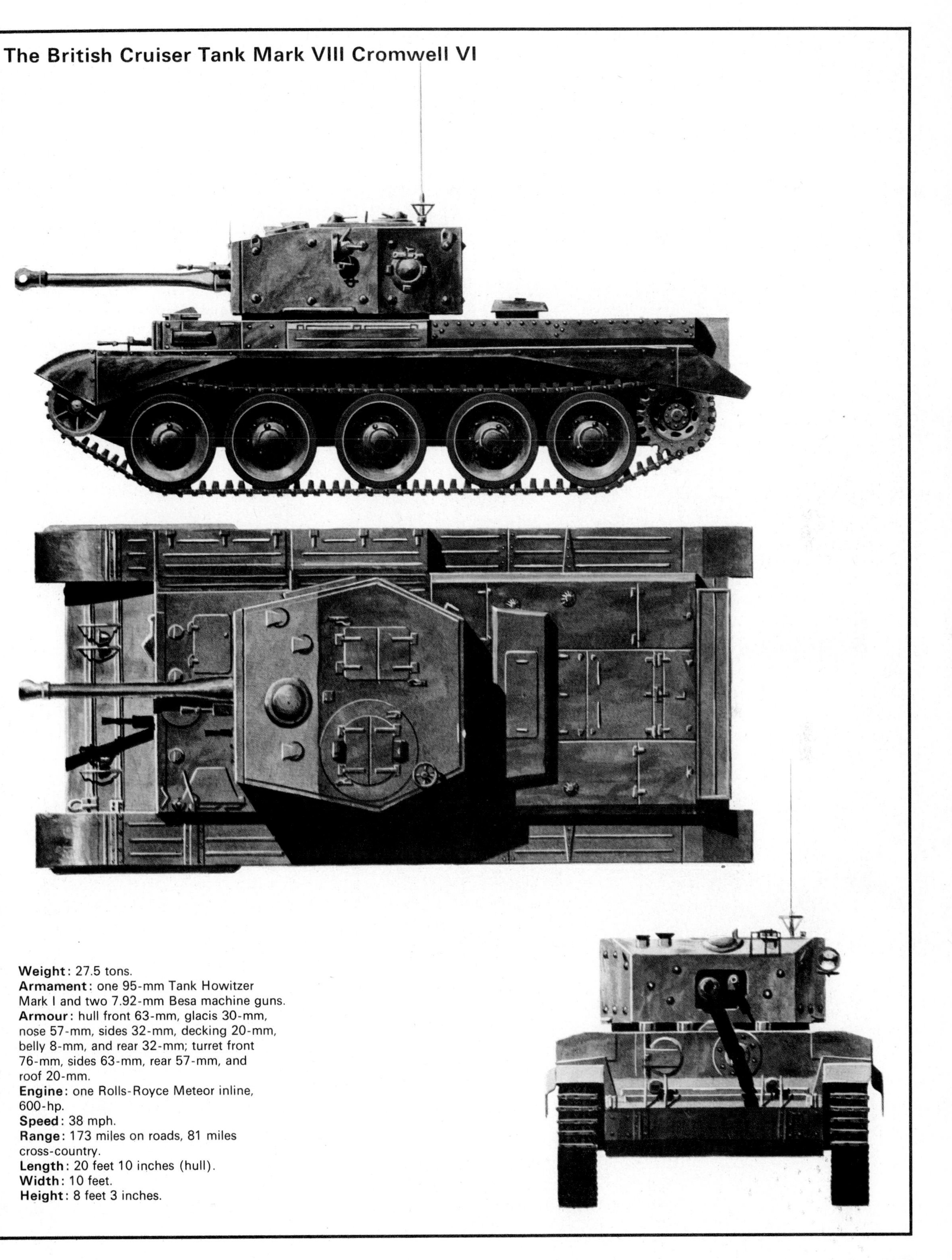

The British Cruiser Tank Mark VIII Cromwell VI

Weight: 27.5 tons.
Armament: one 95-mm Tank Howitzer Mark I and two 7.92-mm Besa machine guns.
Armour: hull front 63-mm, glacis 30-mm, nose 57-mm, sides 32-mm, decking 20-mm, belly 8-mm, and rear 32-mm; turret front 76-mm, sides 63-mm, rear 57-mm, and roof 20-mm.
Engine: one Rolls-Royce Meteor inline, 600-hp.
Speed: 38 mph.
Range: 173 miles on roads, 81 miles cross-country.
Length: 20 feet 10 inches (hull).
Width: 10 feet.
Height: 8 feet 3 inches.

Heinrici kept his 18th *Panzergrenadier*, 11th *"Nordland"* S.S. *Freiwilligen Panzergrenadier*, and 23rd *"Nederland"* S.S. *Freiwilligen Panzergrenadier* Divisions, composed of Norwegian, Danish, Dutch, and Belgian volunteers.

Finally, O.K.H. kept control of XXXIX Panzer Corps, but as Hitler's intuition told him that the Russians' main attack would be directed not against Berlin, but along the Görlitz–Dresden–Prague axis, he handed over this corps to Field-Marshal Schörner and put LVI Panzer Corps, which was considerably weaker, in the rear of Army Group "Vistula".

Roosevelt dies

On April 12, Franklin Roosevelt's sudden death seemed to Hitler like a long awaited and providential miracle, comparable in every respect to the divine intervention which had eliminated the Tsarina Elizabeth and saved Frederick II, who had been on the point of taking poison at the worst moment of the Seven Years' War. Hitler thought he would not only defeat the Russians at the gates of Berlin, but that the English, American, and Soviet forces would become inextricably confused in Mecklenburg and Saxony, German guns would fire themselves, and he would remain master of the situation.

The Russians, according to the message sent to Eisenhower by Stalin, were using only "secondary forces" against Berlin in this last battle of the war on the Eastern Front. These "secondary forces" totalled at least three army groups or fronts, consisting of 20 armies, 41,000 mortars and guns, 6,300 tanks, and 8,400 planes in the attack, which started at 0400 hours on April 16. On the 1st Belorussian Front, which broadly speaking was facing the German 9th Army, Marshal Zhukov had ten armies: 3rd and 5th Shock Armies, 8th Guards Army (General V. I. Chuikov), 1st and 2nd Guards Tank Armies (Generals M. E. Katukov and S. I. Bogdanov), the 1st Polish Army (General S. G. Poplavsky), and the 61st, 47th, 8th, and 33rd Armies. He also had eight

▽ *Russian armour/infantry attack. Note the man at the left, carrying a mortar base plate.*

artillery divisions and General S. I. Rudenko's 16th Air Army. His task was to encircle and take Berlin.

On Zhukov's right, Marshal I. S. Konev's 1st Ukrainian Front contained seven armies: 3rd and 5th Guards Armies (Generals V. N. Gordov and A. S. Zhadov), 3rd and 4th Guards Tank Armies (Colonel-General P. S. Rybalko and General D. D. Lelyushenko) 2nd Polish Army (General K. Swierczewski), and 13th and 52nd Armies. He also had seven artillery divisions and Colonel-General K. A. Vershinin's 4th Air Army. After forcing the Neisse, Konev was to exploit his victory along the Bautzen–Dresden axis, but in case Zhukov's thrust slowed down, he was to be prepared to converge his mobile troops on Berlin and take part in the encirclement and assault on the city.

To the right of Zhukov, the 2nd Belorussian Front (Marshal K. K. Rokossovsky) had five armies (2nd Shock, and 19th, 65th, 70th, and 49th) with four tank or mechanised corps, and Colonel-General S. A. Krasovsky's 2nd Air Army. On April 20, Rokossovsky was to attack on the Schwedt–Neustrelitz axis, drive the 3rd *Panzerarmee* to the Baltic, and link up with Field-Marshal Montgomery's forces. Although Telpukhovsky as usual does not state the number of Soviet divisions taking part in this campaign, they may be assessed at 140 divisions or their equivalent. The Germans had 37 weakened divisions to take the first blow, including the 4th *Panzerarmee,* which faced the 1st Ukrainian Front on the Neisse. Another difficulty was caused by the fact that the defence was extremely short of fuel and munitions, and the German troops were seriously undertrained. Moreover, as Telpukhovsky points out, Soviet planes had complete air supremacy. Busse, for instance, only had 300 fighters, all desperately short of fuel, to oppose Zhukov's 16th Air Army.

The final appeal

As Zhukov and Konev started the attack, the German troops were handed out Adolf Hitler's last order of the day, which included the following passages:

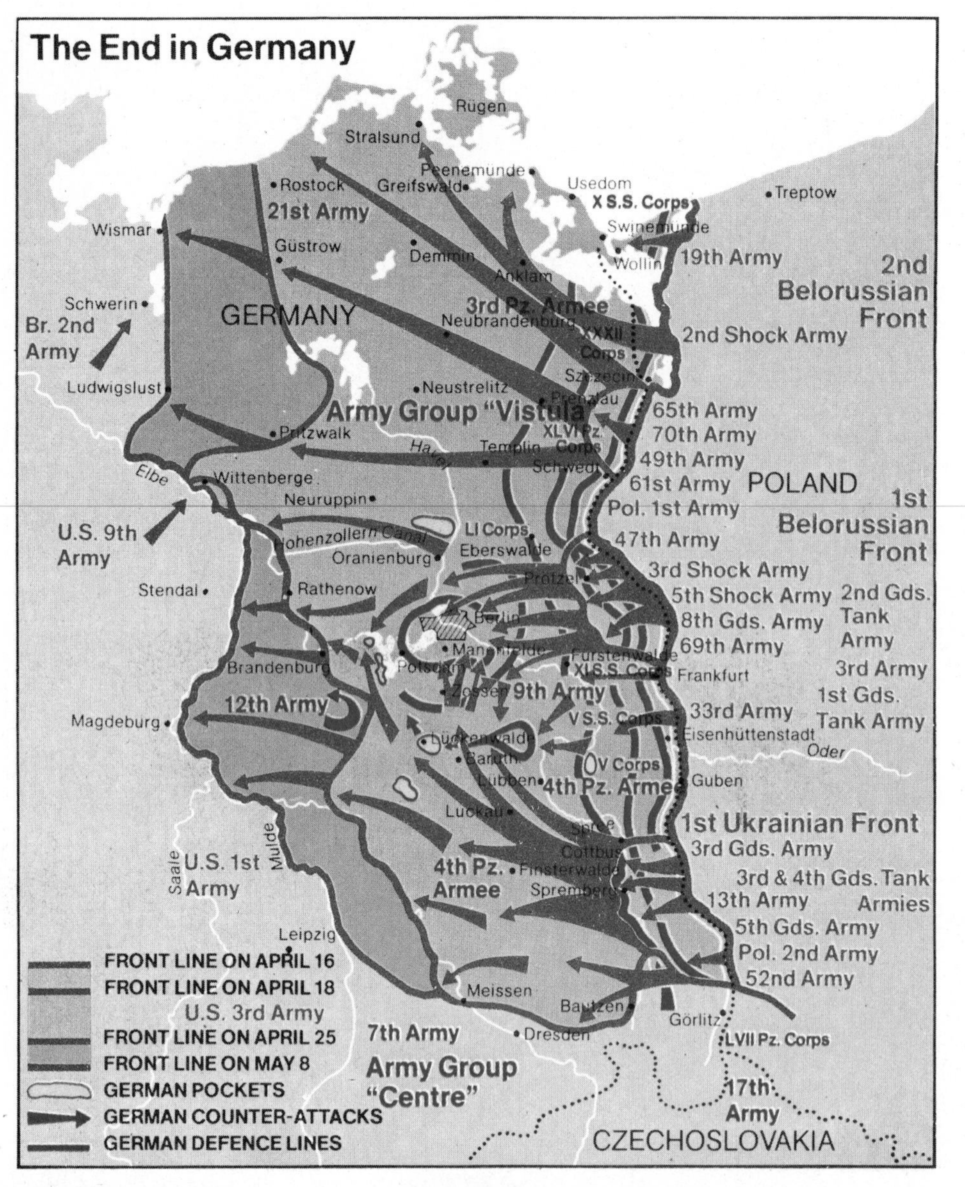

"For the last time, the deadly Jewish-Bolshevik enemy has started a mass attack. He is trying to reduce Germany to rubble and to exterminate our people. Soldiers of the East! You are already fully aware now of the fate that threatens German women and children. Whilst men, children, and old people will be murdered, women and girls will be reduced to the rôle of barrack-room whores. The rest will be marched off to Siberia."

But the Führer had provided the means to put a stop to this terrible assault; everything was ready for meeting it, and the outcome now depended on the tenacity of the German soldiers. He therefore wrote: "If every soldier does his duty on the Eastern Front in the days and weeks to come, Asia's last attack will be broken, as surely as the Western enemy's invasion will in spite of everything finally fail.

"Berlin will remain German. Vienna will become German again and Europe will never be Russian!"

At the same time the Soviet soldiers in the line were told: "The time has come to free our fathers, mothers, brothers, sisters, wives, and children still languishing under the Fascist yoke in Germany. The time has come to draw up the balance sheet of the abominable crimes perpetrated on our soil by the Hitlerite cannibals and to punish those responsible for these atrocities. The time has come to inflict the final defeat on the enemy and to draw this war to a victorious conclusion."

△ *The Allies crush Germany.*
▷ *Russian armour on the move.*